P.O.W.E.R.

How God Will Disarm Your Stalker and Give You the Power Back!

Dr. Makayla Anderson

Disclaimer

The following story is 100% true and corroborated by factual events and has been well documented by the courts, newspapers and television reports. However, the names of people involved and some places have been changed for protection and privacy purposes.

ACKNOWLEDGEMENTS

There are so many people to thank, but I must first acknowledge God, my Father. Romans 8:37 says, "We are more than a conqueror" which means we not only achieve victory, but we are overwhelmingly victorious. God reminds me not to be afraid!

I thank Bishop Black and the members at Faith Tabernacle who prayed and encouraged me throughout this entire ordeal. I am forever grateful to my church families at New Life, The Salvation Army, Seacoast, Revival Team Out Reach Ministries and Victory Baptist.

I thank my family for supporting me and standing by my side. I cherish my friends and neighbors who heard my cries and reminded me that love always wins and there is no room for evil.

A special acknowledgment goes out to Jane, the investigator assigned to this case. Without her, my case would have fallen through the cracks.

DEDICATION

This story is for and about the hurt, pain and tribulation of thousands of women and men who will come after me.

This book is an assist, a helping hand or a shoulder for when you need to turn to someone who understands.

I dedicate this book to those thousands, perhaps millions of people who have, are currently, or will experience the vile crime of stalking.

With this book, I only mean to say that I understand. I know. I get it.

I pray my story will help give you some ideas, or even just one spark that may help you get through the struggle and allow the good Lord to give you your power back!

TABLE OF CONTENTS

INTRODUCTION

Sunday, January 19, 2020
Preparing for Court

I wasn't exactly sure of who I could or should ask to go to court with me. I was not scared, not really, but this was a critical day in my life and perhaps the defining moment in a six-year long nightmare.

After more than six years of stalking me, abusing me, terrorizing me, and trying to kill me and my family, this day in court would finally put an end to the horrific attacks because the court would be convicting my narcissistic psychotic ex, James Oden and sending him to prison. Then again, perhaps the real nightmare would be just beginning, and they would let him go; let that monster loose on the world and free to seek out his sick revenge on me.

I knew all too well that if the law allowed him to go this time, if they let him off, if they let him out to continue his barbaric sadistic attacks, this time he would be successful; this time he would finally kill me and anyone who got in the way. I needed someone to come with me, someone for support, but who?

I thought about my dear sweet mother who had already expressed the desire to be there with me in the courtroom, but because she was seventy-seven years old, I was naturally concerned.

I could only imagine what she might do if she laid eyes on the fiend who had tormented us for all of those years. She could have a heart attack or something.

Finally, I decided to shut off my brain and let the Lord advise me then instantly the Holy Spirit put my friend Donna on my mind and I sent her an email asking if she would accompany me to court the following day to court.

After hitting the "Send" button, I realized that I really didn't know Donna very well. We were acquaintances, but other than the fact that she worked at the courthouse as a volunteer, I didn't know her at all.

I felt that asking her to join me on such an intimate and life changing event might have been out of place and she would probably feel the same.

I sat back down at my computer and started to email Donna and retract the invitation, then decided to just call her, when my cell phone rang. To my surprise, it was Donna.

Donna told me that she had been tracking my court case and was waiting for me to contact her. She said that her schedule was open for the week and she would love to accompany me to court. All I could say was, *Thank You, Lord!* He knew what I needed.

Monday, January 20, 2020
On My Way

It was a ten-hour drive from Mississippi to the South Carolina court for this trial and I knew it was time I would need to listen to enough spiritual CDs to prepare my head, heart, and attitude. Sure enough, after dropping off the pets at the kennel, I hit the road with Joel Olsteen and K-Love Radio.

Along the way a sense of fear and apprehension seized me and I felt like Daniel about to be thrown into the lion's den. Recognizing this as an obvious and expected mental attack of the enemy, I initiated my pre-planned defense of K-Love Radio's prayer line on speed-dial.

I called and requested prayer for victory on the upcoming legal battlefield and drove the rest of the way with a sense of a hedge of protection surrounding me.

Tuesday, January 21, 2020, 9:00 A.M.
The Pretrial

Donna and Don, another courthouse volunteer, both greeted me as I stepped off the elevator on the second floor of the 14th Judicial Circuit Court

Strangely, instead of the smiles and enthusiastic looks of positivity and hope I expected to receive, I saw an outward feeling of dread on both of their faces. Donna tried to hide it with a bit of a forced smile, but the facade was not enough to conceal the truth.

"What's going on?" I asked before even saying hello.

Don put his arm around my shoulder and looked around as if making sure no one would overhear what he was about to say.

"We need to talk," He whispered. "It's important."

The three of us walked over to an area next to a nearby water fountain and away from other people and reporters in the narrow hallway.

Don's job as volunteer was to listen to the phone calls of the inmates in the jail. He, like six other volunteers were assigned to listen and become familiar with the calls of particular prisoners, and one of the prisoners assigned to Don was James Oden.

He knew he was not supposed to reveal to me or to anyone outside of his supervisors what he had heard, but Don was sure that what he had heard was serious and even life threatening.

"James is trying to set you up!" Don screamed in a whisper.

Don went on to explain that James had a lengthy conversation with someone. He told this person that I had a key to his dive shop and that it was me who had gone in and placed all of the evidence the police found that ultimately sent him to jail.

As ludicrous as this was, it sounded like something James would do and at first, I didn't worry about it. But Don went on to explain that James, of course aware that someone was listening to and recording his phone calls, acted as if this was something that he just remembered.

Don said James acted and sounded like a devastated victim, saying things like, "I can't believe she would do something like that to me" and "I can't believe she set me up..." and "All I did was love her..."

Don told me that when he informed his supervisor about the call, the supervisor said it may be used as evidence.

My heart sank and time momentarily froze. Then the frozen time moved on to my spine and sent a frosty chill through my whole body.

Just then, the doors to Courtroom #3 opened and people filed in. Sitting there in the last row, Don on one side of me and Donna on the other, I looked up and saw James walk in and it all came back to me. In an instant, I relived the whole six-year long nightmare.

The pretrial began on the exact path that Don had painted, with James' lawyer doing everything he could to have the case dismissed. This wolf in predator's clothing even motioned to dismiss the case on the basis that the evidence was tainted because the lead investigating officer, Jane Sloan and I were intimately involved with each other.

Don, Donna and I just looked at one another in a cloud of surprise at the unmitigated gall of the suggestion that Jane and I were having an affair, but it did not come as a shock to any of us.

The real blow though came when the judge, presented with a motion to suppress, stated that she would not allow any evidence going back any further than the last six months.

When I heard this, I thought it had it be a joke; after all, James was in jail for most of that time. The only thing that could be presented were the few creepy things he did; like the three last so-called greeting cards he left me, and videos of him driving around my mother's house.

We would have only six-months-worth of evidence to describe over six years of torment. This was not good. Add to this, the possibility they would also use the taped phony phone calls from James' incarceration and this really was not looking good.

My stomach turned green and I took in a deep breath in effort to calm my insides so I would not have to rush out of the courtroom and dry heave my insides out.

This was it.

CHAPTER 1
JUNE 2018
P.O.W.E.R.

The loud, thunderous chopping and pounding of the helicopter blades as they carved through the air gave me the thought of God almighty, beating down on the building with His fist, as the entire hotel seemed to tremble in the constant concussion.

"Vu-Vump-Vu-Vump-Vu-Vump!" the helicopter rhythmically bellowed as it came closer to the ground, and I could clearly understand why they nicknamed those things, *Choppers*; it was literally chopping up the air.

My mother, my sister, and I ran to the nearest window just as a powerful search light beamed down from the flying fortress and began slowly and methodically sweeping over the wooded area nearby. For a moment, I wondered why they would use the spotlight in the daytime, but then I could see that the light did indeed illuminate the heavily shaded area it searched.

The chopping diminished slightly and the spotlight dimmed a bit as the chopper moved away, but it all came roaring back as the helicopter circled around.

Adding to the whirlwind in the air, the "Wah, wah, wah…" howling of police car sirens rose up as a kaleidoscope of red and blue lights appeared to come from everywhere and nowhere.

Suddenly, dogs barking pierced through the commotion and we could hear the static of police radios in the distance. Apparently, they were closing in on their suspect.

My phone buzzed, hummed or whatever you want to call it, as it was on vibrate mode and made a distinct clatter on the wooden dresser. I grabbed it and saw a new text. It was an alert from the BSCO (Beaufort County Sherriff's Office).

"Expect Heavy Law Enforcement Presence near 2230 Parkway Drive. Officers have an active warrant on file and the subject was reported fleeing in the area near Lost Island Rd. and Little Creek Rd. along the powerlines.....The fleeing subject was seen wearing a ball cap and a light blue shirt..."

Dogs barking, helicopter thundering and searching, police shouting, sirens blaring and radios chattering; the whole scene played out like a chaotic episode of "Cops: Any City U.S.A.", or the end of a gruesomely violent bank robbery movie where the cornered lone gunman, having no escape and prison-style spotlights dancing over him, vows to go out in a blaze of glory.

But this was not some blood and guts action movie and this wasn't a ridiculous, racially slanted syndicated television series, and the suspect was not an *America's Most Wanted* bank robber, child abductor, or serial killer.

This was Real Life 101, and the suspect was my ex-boyfriend; a mentally unstable, narcissistic, dangerous and violent, serial stalker.

A sudden chilling terror struck me and I felt myself tremble.

I hunched my shoulders as in effort to protect my head from some unknown incoming object, as a freezing cold sense of fear ran down my back like someone poured an orange bucket of Gatorade and ice over my head after a winning game. The three of us half expected to hear gunfire erupt at any moment and see bullets come flying though the walls in any direction.

My mother, sister, and I hugged each other and stood there, nervously watching and anxiously waiting. This is it, I thought. "It will all be over soon. It will all be over soon…"   I kept telling myself, or actually, praying to myself. "Praise God, it will be over soon."

Investigator Jane

Two days earlier, I had received a call from my investigator, Jane, who told me that she had obtained the warrants.   I affectionately refer to Jane as *my investigator,* as if she were my personal P.I.   Jane is actually Corporal Jane Sloan of the Beaufort County Sheriff's Department.

When I met Jane, I had already talked to a dozen or more police officers from all over the place. While most at least, seemed to have my best interest at heart, and put on the appearance of trying to do their job and apprehend and file charges against my assailant; Jane was the only one who showed genuine empathy for me and my plight.

At the time of this writing, the *crime of stalking* is considered something new even though the action itself is not new. Deranged, narcissists and anti-social criminals have been committing this crime, and getting away with it, since the beginning of time. But the criminal offense of *stalking*, and the actual creation of criminal laws against such crimes, is a new area of law. Your average cop is simply not someone who has the motivation to break precedent or do something that has never been done before. However, there was something different about Jane, something more, and I believe that God directed our lives to cross paths. She had the passion and dedication, as well as the knowledge and legal access that I so desperately needed.

Jane was fantastic; smart, diligent, and thorough. She had compiled a detailed seven-page affidavit that described all of James' activities over the last few years and submitted it along with her requests for the warrants.

The result was that she was able to secure a warrant for James' arrest, and equally as important, a warrant for *Search and Seizure*. This was huge, as the police could now confiscate James' computers, smart phones, and any technology he used to hack into my life.

Finally, we could get some proof of the cruel cyber abuse that he continuously inflicted on me in every way from Facebook pages to cell phone hacks, to email intrusions and everything you can imagine.

Jane told me that after reading the report, the magistrate judge summed up the whole thing in the most technical, legalistic words of jurisprudence: "This guy is nuts!"

Jane then began to explain her plan of action in apprehending James the next day. James owned and operated a dive shop near the water's edge on Lost Island where he sold deep-sea diving and other related gear and accessories.

Jane was going to station two officers to "stake-out" the dive shop, starting at 7:00 a.m. Jane would then keep a clandestine eye on the place as she waited in her unmarked car down the street, in case James decided to make a run for it.

She would park in the perfect place, covering what was the only way out of the area, unless James made the insane decision to turn in the other direction and dive off the pier into the Atlantic and try his luck at a swimming get-a-away.

With police on stake out and Jane under cover down the street, when James showed up for what he thought was a normal day of business, they would have him virtually surrounded.

All I could do was imagine everything, as I sat in the hotel room, waiting on updates from Jane. For a moment, I briefly envisioned the two police, in their squad car; one of them gripping a shotgun, the other, listening to the walkie-talkie, and Jane down the street, behind black, mirror-like sunglasses. Good Lord, I thought, as my heartbeat began pounding so hard it was physically shaking my body; this really is turning out like a bad movie.

But then my thoughts abated, and my heart calmed as the overwhelming warmth and love of God poured over me. The Holy Spirit, in a way that only God can communicate, let me know that I had nothing to fear.

After a short time, the two Sheriff's officers outside the dive shop noticed that James was already in the shop, and they and Jane strategized a plan to go in and arrest him.

However, as slimly snakes often do, somehow, James managed to give the authorities the slip. He slithered out the back door, nearly in a belly crawl, and at an angle that made it difficult to see him. Like a mouse, or better yet, a rat, he burrowed through the trash and garbage, using the refuse for cover, and disappeared into the deep woods.

When she called to let me know that James had escaped, Jane, sensing that the news would unnerve me, assured me that they would catch him quickly and told me that I needed to concentrate of writing my "victim's statement."

She had advised me before that this statement, which I was to read at James' arraignment, was critical to making sure the judge would deny him bail, or at least make it so high that James would remain in custody. Jane insisted that I get the victim's statement ready immediately, implying that James' arrest was imminent.

However, though I really could appreciate Jane's empathy and kindness, I knew she was trying to help me get my mind off the fact that an unhinged sociopath had escaped capture and was on his way to kill me.

Knowing that the cops were closing in, knowing that they now had all the evidence they needed, knowing that he was already in violation of his 3-year probation from the previous conviction for harassment of me, which would add at least three years to all of the other pending and piling up charges; in his disturbed mind, he would have no choice but to kill me and probably those I loved, as well.

The search for James Oden was on. I wondered if he might end up in a shootout with the police. I was pretty certain that like any prudent terrorist, James was armed.

He would never use such weapons on me, though he might shoot or stab my family; but not me. He made that clear before. He made it clear that for me, it was personal. He made it clear that with me, it was intimate. With me it would not even be murder, it would be love.

On second thought, I figured there was no way James would get into a gunfight with the cops; he would never take a stand like that. If there was a way he could cower and slither his way out, he would choose that road or back alley, rather than a *mano e mano* fight to the death.

Then, almost as abruptly as it started, the commotion outside came to a halt. The helicopter faded off and did not circle back and the police sirens stopped. It was suddenly quiet, too quiet. I'm not sure which was more nerve-wracking; the riotous commotion or the sudden quiescence.

Then, I knew that they had caught him; I just knew. I knew because God put a song on my heart, an old Gospel classic and one of my favorites, "Victory is Mine," by Dorothy Norwood.

Sharon, a good friend and prayer warrior, had suggested that I listen to the uplifting song in times of stress. But this was not a time of stress, it was a time of assurance and the lyrics played in my head with full choir and orchestra.

"Victory is mine, Victory is mine,
Victory today is mine.
I told Satan to get thee behind,
Victory today is mine!"

A few minutes later, Jane called with the news that James had been apprehended. I later found that as Jane and other officer's began to backtrack and trace James' get-a-way trail through the woods, they found a large, blue plastic storage container, which I later identified as one that James had stolen from me. In it, James had a .45 semi-automatic handgun, a semi-automatic rifle with a scope, air rifle and two powerful crossbows, with arrows.

The crossbows, I guessed, were for me. In his own sick way, to James, the bow and arrow could represent cupid and his innocent, insatiable, so-called love for me. So of course, he would shoot me through the middle of my heart with a crossbow and we would be tethered together; together forever.

I don't know for sure if that's what he had in mind, but that is how he thinks. For those reading this, who believe that your stalker, your ex-intimate partner, could never be physically violent to you or hurt you; think again.

Power Stolen

The stalker highjacks your power. The stalker drains and sucks the power from you like a vampire leech attached to your skin.

The stalker; the selfish, and dangerous criminal, draws the life energy from you until you become a shell of a person, a perpetually frightened and paranoid puppet who has to always look over your shoulder, literally check in the closets and under the bed for monsters and have a more than justifiable fear of the dark.

I am not ashamed to tell you, quite honestly, that this is the level I had sunk to after years of being the victim of stalking. I am not ashamed to tell you because I know that there are many people out there, many of you reading this book right now, that are at that point; the point where you have become powerless.

However, this book is not about the power you lose, nor is this book about the power the stalker has. This book is about getting *your* power back. This book is about how to get your power back and regain control as you totally disarm your stalker. This book is about victory!

You might have noted the "Dr." before my name on the cover of the book. However, I am not a psychiatrist or therapist of any kind, so I don't claim to be an expert on Narcissistic Personality Disorder or the mind of the stalker.

However, I believe and pray that by sharing some of my story, some of what happened to me and what I went through, you will be able to see and learn as I did. You will learn more about the laws and the lack thereof, more of the mentality of the person haunting you, and most importantly, I pray that you will discover a few ways to deal with the situation and regain control of your life. That is what this book is about.

Now, let me also tell you what this book is not.

This book is not a *white paper*. It is not a psychological study, a textbook or a thesis. This book is simply an explanation of what I believe will help you escape the stalker's prison and recover. This book is simply part of *my story*; that actually, has not ended quite yet, not even as of the day of this writing.

The most essential thing that I found is that this battle is one that is not merely of flesh and blood. That is, fending off a hostile, deranged, and dangerous stalker is a fight against more than the stalker; be it a him or her. It is a battle against evil in its simplest and purest form.

You have to understand that the mind of the stalker is not one of rationale, though it may seem as if the reasoning behind your pursuer's actions are obvious.

You may come to believe that your stalker's motivations are understandable; over-the-top and outrageous, yes, but understandable, nonetheless.

You may think that although this person may be a little unbalanced, that he or she is only reacting to hurt and pain.

You may think that the contemptible and dangerous behavior he or she displays is due to normal human emotions such as jealousy, rejection, dependence, fear of loss, loss of love, or something as simple as the pain of a broken heart. However, this is not true.

Over the last few years, I have done a lot of reading and studying on the stalker mentality and the actions and behaviors of such are anything but normal. These actions can include physical as well as verbal domestic abuse; traditional stalking in person, cyber stalking all over the internet and social media, gang stalking and harassment, which are all serious criminal offenses.

Being on the receiving end of these offenses, for me, were the most frightening and debilitating experiences of my life. My perpetrator's behaviors and malicious acts temporarily left me catatonic and withdrawn.

No, such actions are not normal; they are evil and more than mere flesh and blood. I stress this because I found that normal weapons do not work. Unless you intend to get a gun and simply take the matter into your own hands, and end the situation with the pull of a trigger; then you need different types of weapons.

Please don't misunderstand me; I am not saying that you should not be armed and ready to defend yourself. Lord knows, my two closest friends and I, *Mr. and Mrs. Smith and Wesson*, have stayed up many nights just waiting for an unsuspecting James to peak his head in the door. I believe that I would not have hesitated to have taken my .44 Magnum and blown his head clean off.

If a *.44 Magnum* sounds familiar, you might be thinking of the cannon sized pistol that Dirty Harry used in the 1971 hit movie of the same name. Come to think of it, Dirty Harry actually used those very words in the movie, when he said to a bad guy, "*...this is a 44 Magnum, the most powerful handgun in the world and will blow your head clean off...*" Of course, Harry said it in a much more dark and scratchy voice than I can write.

However, that is the last thing that I wanted to happen, and it is the last thing *you* want to happen, and the last thing you want to have to live with. Guns are not the weapon of choice for this fight.

For this battle, you need to arm yourself with the spiritual weapons of God.

Hold On!

Before those of you who may not have a relationship with God or believe like I do, decide to close this book, let me tell you one more thing this book is not.

This book is not a Bible lesson. I am no more a preacher, a pastor, or a Bible scholar, than I am a psychiatrist. This book is not a scriptural study, or a religious recruitment tool meant to persuade or proselytize. Once again, this is just part of *my* story and what worked for me.

I might add though, that if you are here, now, reading this book, and you have *not* tried God; then doing so may be something think about.

Power Restored

Whatever it is that you have been through, whatever level of powerlessness you feel you may have sunk to, and whatever degree of depression, despair, and despondency you may have reached, you can rest assured that you can, and you will, get it all back. You can get your power back, totally disarm your stalker, and regain the control and dignity in your life that you deserve.

On my road to regaining control and getting my power back, I noticed several tactics and processes that really seemed to work in the course of solving some stalker issues and challenges. I am not talking about some magic tricks or supernatural tips that miraculously made my stalker nightmare disappear. I am referring to some simple, straightforward, and practical steps that I took, and when I put them all together, they spelled victory.

Then, between the good Lord leading me, and my empathic desire to prevent anyone from ever going through the things that I endured, or at the very least, help someone avoid some of the lowest pitfalls I suffered, and to help them recover a bit faster, I decided to write this book.

I believe these steps can really help you avoid, fight back, and overcome. It seemed to me it may be easier to follow and remember them, so I used the acronym, P.O.W.E.R.

Let me give you a brief overview of P.O.W.E.R., and then I'll take you through each step while explaining what happened to me and how each step helped me so much.

P.O.W.E.R. =

P = Pray and Watch

O = Open Up

W = Whole Amour of God

E = Exonerate

R = Regain Control

P = Pray and Watch

Prayer is the most critical and important first step, not only in your quest to regain control of your life, but in everything.

As promised, I am not going to turn this into a Bible lesson or proselytize, but I truly believe prayer is essential.

You need to pray continuously, or until you feel in your heart and in your spirit, that your prayers have been answered. Also, it is important to get others involved in praying for you as well.

Do not think for one moment however, that this is all about *only* prayer. No, no, no. This is not a situation where you just leave it all up to God and wash your hands of the issue. When I say pray and watch, that does not mean pray and sit back and wait.

You want to pray, true, but you also want to *stand guard* and watch. You have to watch your back and that can include being ready and armed if necessary.

In this chapter, I will explain how this step helped me; how I prayed and prayed, but how I definitely stood watch and stayed armed to the teeth.

O = Open Up

This may be challenging for you, but you need to talk to someone and get others involved in what is happening. Your stalker's actions often appear so implausible that they are difficult for some people to believe; all the while the stalker takes steps to appear innocent and even as a victim.

Also, like any accusation of a sexual nature, there is the real fear of not having people believe you, or of the whole ordeal becoming public and a dozen other outrageous and painful consequences of coming forward.

Please understand that your silence is one of your stalker's biggest assets. You must open up and tell someone; join a church, get involved in ministries, contact officials in the business such as domestic coordinators or counselors. Do something!

W = Whole Armour of God

Now that you have prayed, are *watching your six*, as they say, and have involved other people in your plight, you need to put on the *whole armour of God*.

If you are not familiar with the *Armour of God* as described in the Bible, you are going to like this.

As I mentioned, this is not a fight against mere flesh and blood, and in the chapter, we'll go over your recommended *battlefield attire*, complete with shield and sword!

E = Exonerate

To exonerate means to forgive, to absolve, to pardon. No matter what, to fully recover and regain your POWER, you are going to have to forgive.

You are going to have to forgive your stalker and you will probably need to forgive yourself as well. Forgive yourself for what, you might ask?

Well for one, you will need to forgive yourself for the horrible fates that you prayed would happen to your stalker. Don't worry, it's only natural to hope that the person pursuing you gets run over by a truck, but you will need to come to terms with that later.

This forgiveness will have to be for real and from the heart, not just lip service where you say that you have forgiven, but live in a state of denial.

Forgiveness is easier said than done and I will share some helpful thoughts on things that helped me, but you have to forgive before you can ever be truly free.

R = Regain Control

Finally, the R in P.O.W.E.R stands for Regain Control. Although that R could easily stand for renew, refresh, reborn, reenergize, or restart. In any case, it is time to celebrate and thank God, *in advance even*, for you getting your power back and truly moving on.

Believe it or not, this step will not be as easy or automatic and natural as you may think.

After being imprisoned by fear and intimidation, after years of justifiable paranoia, looking over your shoulder, triple checking your doors and windows, jumping out of your socks at the sound of thunder or a when a car backfires, it is not easy to be normal again.

In this chapter I will share with you some of the things that helped me see straight once I was back in control.

Important Resources

In addition to giving you some important resources and information as we go, in the rear of the book I also give you a more detailed listing of essential telephone numbers, groups and organizations to contact that can help you.

Also, if you have trouble finding someone to talk to so that you can take advantage of the second step, O = Open Up, you will have information on how to communicate with me. I'd love to talk with you because I know where you are coming from. I have literally "been there and done that".

It's Not Your Fault

Before we get into the POWER plan though, I need to give you a brief overview of how I got to this point, how it all started.

Often, staking victims believe that somehow, they are totally or at least in some part, responsible for the stalker's unpredictable and violent behavior.

It is common to think that *"If I only did not shun him..."* or *"Maybe when I refused her offer, I did it too coldly..." "Something I did made him or her snap."*

However, nothing could be farther from the truth.

While you will feel some guilt and experience a sense of blame, it is not true. Yes, you, like I did, probably can look back and see many mistakes that you made during and before the stalking began.

You will look back and realize that in the beginning there were dozens of "red flags" clearly alerting you that there were problems with this intimate partner, even before you became intimate.

Yes, you will look back and see the places where you zigged where you should have zagged, and maybe if you had, all of the nightmares that you have lived through might not have happened.

You will reflect back and wonder how you could have been so stupid. You will think "My goodness, how could I have ever done that? How could I have ever fell for this…" etc.

Please understand that this is all hindsight and it is true that hindsight is indeed 20—20 vision. These, almost completely self-imposed guilt trips are nothing more than an illusion. They are absolute nonsense, so please don't let them get you down.

Unless you had a perfectly functioning crystal-ball at the time, there is no way you could have known the outcome of anything that you did or did not do.

Also, no matter how much it may appear to be so, the fact is that you cannot, and could not ever, control and create the actions of another person. Everyone has a free will and a mind of their own, even though that is often hard to believe.

I also said that the guilt trip is *almost* completely self-imposed because some of it does not come from you. Some of it is societal, in that there are so-called standards that we, often unwittingly, judge ourselves against. Since this book for people of all ages, I will not get into what I think about the so-called social order, and level of decorum or moral values. Just throw the whole idea out of your mind.

Lastly on this subject of imposed feelings of guilt after the fact, is that much of it comes from the devil. Once again, don't panic, but this is what I believe. The devil's job is to make you feel bad and horrible and to judge and accuse you. It is clear in the Bible that the devil is the accuser of the people.

Believe that or not, in either case, when those thoughts of guilt cross your mind, you need to squash them. You are human and you will make the same type of mistakes that most humans make. As you will soon see, I made a bunch of them.

So that is the construct; the framework of *POWER: How God Will Disarm Your Stalker and Give You the Power Back!*

Now, let's get ready to get to it, and I'll see you later as we all sing *Victory is Mine!*

MARRIED, DIVORCED

AND

THE BIRTH OF A STALKER

Let me start from the beginning and give you the *Readers Digest-Cliff Notes* version of what led me to this point and how it all developed.

I would love to begin this story by telling you that I had a perfect childhood. However, with a terminally absent father, and an overworked mother who single-handedly raised me, my upbringing was anything but perfect.

I was a mediocre student in what I thought was a mediocre Catholic school in anything but a mediocre city. I grew up in San Francisco, California with no real desire to go to college. After high school, I bounced from one meaningless to job to the next. During those wandering years, I had two beautiful boys; John and Anthony, who became the center on my life and I decided it was time to grow up. I enlisted in the U.S. Marine Corps at the age of twenty.

During my military career, as I finally began to feel like a responsible grown woman, and went to nursing school. In the summer 2008, I met a handsome, very kind, and thoughtful young man who was also a Marine. No, this was not lunatic stalker, James. The Marine was Rob and after courting for a while, certain that I was in love, Rob and I married in March of 2011.

As enlisted personnel in different fields, the military gave my new husband and I different orders and base assignments constantly, so, we had less than what anyone would call a traditional marriage arrangement. After the wedding, we spent much of our married life living apart on different bases in different states.

By 2012, just a little over a year after we were married, Rob took the option of an early retirement from the Marines at only thirty-four years old. I knew that this was a huge mistake and so did Rob's mother. She also knew his drinking pattern and behavior much more than I could ever imagine. She knew what Rob could do with too much time on his hands, but I would find out the hard way.

After only a few months into his retirement, Rob's daily beer consumption reached levels I thought would send any normal person to the emergency room, but it didn't seem to faze him. For him, beer was a nutritional supplement and without it, he would not survive.

I thought it was insane when I began to see him drink eight to ten cans of Bud Light a day, that is, until the end of that year, when he was easily drinking twenty-five to thirty cans a day. Yes, that is *a day* and by himself.

Rob's physical condition was quickly deteriorating, not only in front of my eyes, but everyone noticed. He started losing his hair, he smelled like a distillery, and reeked of old cigarette smoke and chewing tobacco.

I personally never cared for smoking or drinking, let alone chewing tobacco, but I never realized how much those habits disgusted me until my husband wore them like a badge of honor.

By January 2013, I had enough, and every fiber of my being cried out for a change. I became isolated and nervous as depression started to sink in, and I deeply resented Rob for the loneliness he inflicted on me. I vividly remember going to the recycling dumpster and tossing out what seemed like thousands of beer cans and bottles nearly every day.

In February the following year, we saw a sharp increase in home break-ins in our neighborhood, so I decided to get another dog, a German Shepard. I already had my pal "Gator", a Labrador mix, but adding the German Shepard seemed to seal the deal. I mean, I certainly could not count on Rob to be sober in the event of a home invasion.

I named the German Shepard "Apache" and quickly realized that adopting him was more about my longing for love and attention than it was about safety and protection.

At this point, my husband had found a boring job he was very unhappy with and so the cycle began. Wake up in the morning, go to work, home by 4:00 pm, straight to the fridge, open and down a dozen or two cans of beer, and pass out. When I reached the preverbal last straw, I woke up and admitted to myself that this was no way to live.

Summer was approaching and there was one hobby I wanted to revisit which was scuba diving. It had been years since I had been diving and when I noticed a scuba shop close to home, I decided to pay the shop a visit.

I met with the owner, named James. Yes, that's when and where I met him. He was very pleasant, upbeat, and willing to sign me up for the upcoming class, although it wouldn't be until May when I could take that refresher class.

The first night of the class was exciting and invigorating for me. Just being out and doing something that I loved, and meeting new friends was absolutely refreshing. I could feel a coming change as if the sun was coming out from behind the clouds and beginning to shine its warm glow on me. I sat in a class with seven other new students and was determined to develop my new independent life that did not involve a beer-guzzling, chain-smoking Rob.

Rob's behaviors continued to get worse, but now I noticed him constantly texting somebody, especially when he was drunk out of his mind. This was unusual for him since he seldom used any form of technology like emailing or texting, both of which were still relatively new concepts for him. I was taking mental notes and wanted to confront him, but rather than the big fight, one night while he was sleeping, I grabbed his cell phone to find out who was this mystery person. I found that this person was, of course, another woman whom I later found out was his office co-worker.

When Rob's usual inebriated night began wearing off, he searched for his phone and when he realized that I had it, the look on his face let me know that there was no need to ask him a single question about his texting partner. Our wonderful joy ride as a married couple pretty much came to an end that night.

In June, both Rob and I went for a visit to North Carolina, but would spend it a few hundred miles apart from each other as Rob went to Camp Lejeune for a friend's retirement party, and, of course, he had to go by himself.

The funny thing is that he knew that I knew that his girlfriend was also then stationed at Camp Lejeune. It didn't take a rocket scientist to figure out the real party he would be attending, duh. It's funny how stupid people assume that everyone is equally as stupid as they are.

However, I welcomed the freedom and the opportunity and chose to go scuba diving at the Blue Stone Dive Resort in North Carolina, which turned out to be an excellent choice. Even though I traveled alone, my new scuba buddies and I were beginning to bond, this of course, included James.

On my way home, I stopped in Columbia, South Carolina and met up with my best friend Pam. We met at our favorite hangout, Ruby Tuesday and each ordered our usual; the *Ruby Relaxer* for me and a *Mojito* for Pam. I brought her up to date on what was going on in my estranged marriage.

While Pam and I were in deep conversation about the weekend's events, I received a call from the dog kennel. Rob never showed up to pick up our pets as we planned. The dogs would have to stay there another night.

I immediately tried to reach Rob, wondering if he might have been in an accident or had car trouble or something, however, there was no answer. When I finally reached him the next day, at first, he had no explanation and then he told me that he had a stomachache and had to stay at Camp Lejeune for another night. Ah, yes, of course, I could understand that; good grief. That one night, turned into two, then three and then a week.

When he finally came home that Thursday, to my surprise, he told me that he had interviewed for a job and was planning to move to North Carolina. As nonchalantly as if he was talking about the weather, he simple said, "*I* am moving and you are not included."

Although I knew the end of us was coming soon, this still stunned me; it shocked me, shook, and rattled me. I actually didn't know why.

I guessed it was that there was no warning of the actual ending, no discussion; no guilty guts spilling out on the floor, no *it's not you, it's me* statements, no build up to a grand finale, nothing.

My heart sank, my head spun, my eyes were blinking as if I was trying to say something in Morse Code.

As it began to sink in, I wasn't sure whether to jump for joy at the realization of finally getting out of such a horrible relationship, or to cry, for fear that I would have to now survive on what would be an extremely reduced income, or just punch him in the mouth, for the audacity of trying to destroy me by using *goodbye* as a blunt instrument.

I adapted as it all began to marinate in the sauce of reality when he drove off on June 29, 2013, headed to his new life, and I guess his new wife, at Camp Lejeune. I didn't know whether I wanted to call that woman a homewrecker and hurt her, or call her a heroine and hug her.

Rob's departure came with mixed blessings. I no longer had to endure the humiliation and wretched stench of living with an irresponsible alcoholic, cigarette-smoking machine, nor did I need to frequent the recycle dumpster as often to off-load a thousand beer cans and bottles, and I could stop going to Al-Anon meetings; at least I thought.

They were all good blessings and I thanked God.

However, Rob's weaponized sayonara would also create a serious lack of financial resources, and that was a major concern.

At this point, I had honorably served my five years, had discharged from the Marine Corps, and was only working a seasonal job that left me high and dry over the summer, and desperately waiting for the fall. I had to do whatever it was I had to do to survive.

I thought about that 1978 song by Gloria Gaynor, "I Will Survive." I loved, and indeed, I lived the lyrics.

> "Weren't you the one who tried to
> hurt me with *goodbye*?
> Did you think I'd crumble?
> Did you think I'd lay down and die?
> Oh no, not I, I will survive!"

It was so true; Rob definitely tried to hurt me as much as he could with the way he said goodbye, and the way and the timing in which he left, and I have no doubt that he believed I would crumble, lay down, and die. Surprise, buddy! Not I!

I began selling all of Rob's personal stuff. Every week I held a garage sale with a *theme* and the first week was "Florida Gator" week.

Rob had every NCAA football Florida Gator kind of memorabilia you could think of, including pajamas, flip-flops, blankets, posters, and shower curtains.

I sold it all for a quick $150 and the buyer, empathizing with my situation, gave me a $25 tip.

The following week was "Video Game" week. Yes, you guessed it; all of Rob's video games and electronics were on the auction block. I must have raked in $300 that week.

The most profitable week was "Military Surplus" week. A new store that sold all sorts of new and used military surplus had just opened in Savannah and they had plenty of Army supplies, but were limited on Marine Corps items.

I packed my little red Honda Civic to the brim like a Rubik's Cube and paid the military surplus store a visit. I had so many items, I filled six eight-foot tables with drill instructor covers, military uniforms, footlockers, swords, you name it. The owner's eyes bulged out when he saw the little gold mine I had.

After I explained my situation, the owner of the shop did not know how much to offer me, and I could see in his eyes that he was honest and did not want to low-ball me either. So, he took a napkin and tore it in half. He asked me to write down an amount and he would do the same. Then we presented our napkins each with a scribbled amount on it.

He had written $400 and I wrote $600. We agreed on $500. I left Savannah with enough money to pay my mortgage. Not only did it turn out to be a profitable summer, but, I must tell you; it was a blast!

Life was good.

I prayed.

The following summer, 2013, would be one that I would never forget. I was focused and determined to make the best of my life and to celebrate who I was. Simultaneously, my emotions continued to jump up and down like a hospital heart monitor beeped with every heartbeat, announcing that at least the patient was still alive. Sometimes it would just remain on the bottom in a flat-line with one long steady monotone beep, while I went through momentary bouts of abandonment and depression, struggling under the stress of making my money stretch to the end of month.

I longed for companionship, intimacy, and love and that made me nervous; I knew that I was vulnerable. I knew that I was easy prey for whatever wolf in sheep's clothing or wolf in wolf's clothing that came along. While on the one hand, I felt strong, independent, successful, and happy but on the other hand, I felt insecure, fragile, frightened, and exposed.

I felt as if there was a huge neon sign suspended above my head, blinking, "Hey fellas, here's a live one!"

Yes, James and I began to get closer.

James would routinely check on me, inquiring how I was doing and so forth, and I found it easy to confide in him. I found out that he too, was going through a divorce, and, well, you know how misery loves company. I wasn't really looking for another relationship, at least I didn't think that I was, but in any case, James seemed to fit like a glove for what I was missing at the time.

Over time, James proved to be rather romantic. He would often have roses delivered to me and would leave little love notes. I knew this was a mistake and it was too soon, as I was still in the healing process. This is one of those times that I would later look back on and think that I should have been more assertive; I should have put a stop to it, I should have slowed it down.

I should have declined one more time when he invited me to the beach for the twentieth time. Well, I don't know *if-I-could-I-would-I-should-have*, but I did.

Our relationship developed fast, too fast, but we were so compatible with each other that it felt natural. We traveled together on scuba diving trips, joined a dance club, and I met his daughter, Sarah. Sarah and I got along famously. It was like we were teenage sorority sisters, hanging out, and even having sleepovers together. James and I started to become like peas and carrots on a perpetual honeymoon.

By the end of that summer, James had practically moved in with me, as I found out that he had lost his house due to foreclosure, and he was actually living in his little twelve-by-fifteen foot dive shop for a few months. (Bing, Bing, Bing!! Bong, bong, bong! Hello! A Red Flag Here!)

I remember visiting his home before the foreclosure and found that he was bona-fide hoarder as well, with old newspapers, magazines, and who knows what, that served as a two foot thick carpet throughout most of the house. (Bing, Bing, Bing!! Red Flags Waving Again!)

The Beginning of the End

James' divorce was complete, but we were not yet a couple, as I was still trying to track down my ex to make my divorce official, but James and I continued to act-as-if we were one.

The next two years were good; they were fun. We joined the local Shag Dance club, wined, dined, and danced many a night away.

However, I began noticing that to James, that's all that seemed to matter to him. All he really showed any interest in was having fun; dancing, having sex, dining out, scuba diving, and the like.

He was always quick to share in those things, yet any cooperation on other areas like paying the bills, he would conveniently disappear. (Red Flags wearing out for waving!)

At first, I didn't think too much of it, which I know was a colossal mistake. I just thought that he had a rough time in his marriage and needed a break from being responsible for everything; he just needed a short vacation.

But as time went on, it became clear that James just did not, and would not, help with any of the expenses, or do anything that had to do with the household. He never offered to pay or even help with the mortgage, the food, utility bills, anything.

When I would mention such things to him, he would just shrug it off as if the bills would either magically go away or I would take care of them. He was like a child who fully expected his mother to take care of everything for him.

Then, when he made it clear that I was also wasting my time by continually asking him to go to church with me, I had to stop and pinch myself.

That's when the intoxicating ether of passion began to wear off, I woke up, and looked at what I was doing, who I was doing it with, and where I was in my life. My mother and my sister, who I always went to church with, saw the instant change in me and my attitude toward James, and applauded my return to reality.

I don't know when I came around and looked at the many red flags and the huge blatant warnings signs. It was almost as if I was living in some sort of weird dream; a fantasy or a trance of some kind, and then suddenly I swallowed the *Red Pill* and immediately saw through the façade.

I also knew that I was not in love with James. He was fun to be with and we had a lot in common, but it was not love by any stretch of the imagination, and it was time to end this childish charade.

By August 2015, I had listed my house in South Carolina for sale and my son, John was insisting that I move with him to the Gulf Coast. John was moving to Biloxi, MS and urged me to join him, partly out of the desire for my company and partly out of the desire to see me get away from James.

So, as soon as I found a buyer for the house in South Carolina, I bought a little beach house near Biloxi and started to solidify my break from James.

As you might imagine, that is the time when Dr. Jekyll began to reveal the infamous Mr. Hyde and things were about to take a turn for the worst.

I can only wish that I had begun my POWER plan right then.

PRAY AND WATCH

Before the stalking begins and the trouble starts is when you need to go into the first letter in the P.O.W.E.R. movement and that is to Pray and Watch. That is, that you need to pray AND watch.

When you notice that things are about to get ugly, when you notice those little things that you tried to ignore, you need to start praying and watching. If it turns out that your precautions were unwarranted, so be it.

However, it is always better to be prepared than not.

Let me make one thing explicitly clear though; when I say pray, by no means am I talking about putting your head in your lap and waiting for God to fix your problems. I am not talking about burying your head in the sand, ala ostrich or ducking into the sanctuary of your own bosom, ala turtle.

To pray and watch is as much an offensive as well as a defensive stance. To pray and watch is fundamental scripture as well as the foundational basis of faith.

First, the Bible makes it clear of what your stance should be.

"Watch ye therefore, and pray always, that ye may be accounted worthy to escape all these things that shall come to pass, and to stand before the Son of man."
---Luke 21:36 (KJV = King James Version)

In fact, the Bible puts the watching ahead of the praying! Watch and pray so that you can escape those things that will come to pass.

I am so glad that I lived long enough to write this book and share these thoughts and strategies with you.

Though I did indeed survive my stalker, and with the help of God, I took my life back. I certainly did not go about it in the exact way I am able to explain it here.

On one hand, I only wish that I would have started the "P", to Pray and Watch at the first sign, or even before the first sign of trouble, but I did not. If I had heeded the advice in this book at that time, I believe things would have worked out much better and faster. But again, that's hindsight.

On the other hand, I am so glad and thankful to God that I did not know to take the precautions in this book, because I was able to learn them. I was able to learn from my missteps and am now able to tell you how to avoid some of those pitfalls.

To pray and watch or actually to watch and pray, is to be alert at all times; that is 24/7. Does that mean that you have to sleep with one eye open? No, but it does mean to remain vigilant at all times. Look at how a more English friendly Bible translation puts that above verse.

"Keep alert at all times. And pray that you might be strong enough to escape these coming horrors and stand before the Son of Man."
---Luke 21:36 (NLT = New Living Translation)

Keep alert and pray that you might escape the coming horrors. Also, note that it does not say pray that the horrors will not come your way. They *will* come.

It is basic scripture that you take steps to protect yourself and guard against those who seek to harm you. That is for *you* to do, not God. Protecting yourself, or watching your back, is your job. Do your job and God will do His. God will do His job in ensuring that your protections succeed in giving you the victory, but you have to do *something*, you have to be invested.

You must take steps, whatever they may be, to protect yourself. Of course, you keep firmly in mind that God will help you; however, the Lord makes it clear to us that we are to always watch and guard against the evil that lurks among us, and you must be ready to fight.

"Blessed be the Lord my strength which teacheth my hands to war, and my fingers to fight."

---Psalm 144:1 (KJV)

Be sober, be vigilant; because your adversary the devil, as a roaring lion, walketh about, seeking whom he may devour.

---1 Peter 5:8 (KJV)

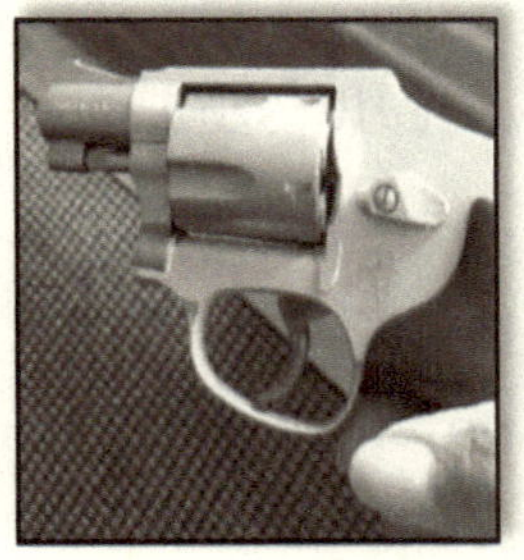

I took those verses quite literally. When I got to Biloxi, James was fully on the prowl, and I bought a nice, sweet little, warm and cuddly Smith and Wesson, snub nose .38 caliber special. I also starting taking shooting lessons, and soon became very comfortable with the handgun.

I am not saying that you have to get a gun, but if you do, I strongly recommend you get lessons on the proper use, safety, and of course, how to hit that at which you shoot.

I might also add that in the state of Mississippi, it is perfectly legal for a woman to carry a pistol in her purse or handbag. That's right; you can carry a loaded gun in your purse with no need for a permit or a concealed license to carry. I had never really been a fan of large oversize purses, but I instantly became one.

Ok, now I was set. I had the snub nose .38 and knew how to use it, and I still had my two faithful dogs, Gator and Apache. That should be enough protection, right?

Gator

Well, for some reason, I wasn't exactly sure. I wondered what would happen if James caught me and cornered me in my living room or on the back porch, and my gun was in the other room; what would I do? I couldn't carry a gun on my person all the time, although the thought had occurred. I figured it would

Apache

be best to simply have another gun in another location in the house.

Mind you, all of this is going on well after I had a million and one iron clad reasons, and proof that such measures would be necessary. James had gotten to the point where he proved to be a legitimate life-threating problem as you will see when I get back into the story in a moment.

Anyway, I bought another .38, but this time I got a regular .38 caliber standard. I seemed to like those

.38s. So, I got yet a third one for another part of the house.

One day at the Gung Ho Shooting Range, I was practicing, or should I say, perfecting my aim; I had gotten pretty good with a .38. I fired off three quick rounds at the silhouetted target some 50 feet away, two in the head and one in the chest. I loved it.

A man in the next booth was also shooting at the targets. But when he fired his gun, it was the loudest thing I had ever heard; it literally sounded like a cannon. When I asked him what in the world was he shooting, he told me it was a .44 Magnum.

"Wow!" I thought, although I think I thought that out loud. Oh, yeah, I remembered, a .44 Magnum; that's the Clint Eastwood, aka *Dirty Harry* gun from the movie of the same name. The man went on to tell me that my choices of the .38's were good picks, especially for a *little woman*, and I was little, all 5-feet of me.

He said, "That .38 you have will help you aim, and it doesn't have too much of kick." He continued as he reloaded the huge revolver.

"If you have a man come running at you, and you hit him in the arm with a .38; you have a man, with a really messed up arm, still trying to coming at you."

He turned toward the targets and fired one shot that nearly shook me to my bones even though I knew it was coming, and he said, "But have a man coming at you and you hit him in the arm with a .44 Magnum; and you have a one-armed man lying on the ground."

I looked down at my .38 and that was it; I got a .44 Magnum. I also found out there were guns that were smaller, lighter and easier to handle, but were still quite lethal, like the .380 Diamond Back. That became one of my favorites; in my hand it felt like it was custom made for me.

Okay, you might be thinking that maybe I went a bit too far, or that I was some kind of a gun nut, or something. Or maybe I just became paranoid and allowed my stalker to make me turn into a recluse. On the contrary. What I did was I took this seriously. I took him, my assailant, very seriously.

If there is only one thing you get from this book, get that. Take this seriously. Do not maintain the thought that "all of this is about love and he won't really harm me."

Please do not think that your stalker is only about talk, because far too many women who have thought that way, have wound up dead. This is serious.

In the end, I only wound up with a total of six handguns, two dogs, a stun gun and three pepper sprays.

Like the scripture says, I stayed alert and on guard. I still prayed and looked to my Lord; I prayed and constantly read the Word of God, but I stayed prepared, as my nightstand, right beside my bed, shows.

Not Against Flesh and Blood

You first step is to pray to watch your back, and protect yourself at all times. Pray and pray until you feel in your heart that your prayers have been answered.

Also, pray that the Lord will help you do what you need to do. Pray that God arms you with more and mighty weapons. He told us that this fight we are in, is not really one against flesh and blood. The fight against evil things and people is not one that is only against people. It is a fight against an enemy that is more than we can deal with.

"For we wrestle not against flesh and blood, but against principalities, against powers, against the rulers of the darkness of this world, against spiritual wickedness in high places."

---Ephesians 6:12 (KJV)

Come on, not even my .44 mag is going to have any affect against *the rulers of darkness*. Listen, you can believe that literally, figuratively, or not at all, but I beseech you to heed it.

Pray that you take on spiritual weapons as well as spiritual protection. Take on the Armour of God and fight in the strength of His might.

"Finally, my brethren, be strong in the Lord, and in the power of his might. Put on the whole armour of God, that ye may be able to stand against the wiles of the devil."

"For we wrestle not against flesh and blood, but against principalities, against powers, against the rulers of the darkness of this world, against spiritual wickedness in high places."

"Wherefore take unto you the whole armour of God, that ye may be able to withstand in the evil day, and having done all, to stand."

---Ephesians 6:10-13 (KJV)

For those of you so inclined, there is a lot more on this amour of God that you will find in your Bible in the sixth chapter of Ephesians. For those of you who are no so inclined, just pray and watch.

Also, yes (and I'll preface this next point by saying that I already know that this is not going to be easy to hear) you need to pray for your stalker or would-be stalker. Let me rephrase that; you need to pray *good* prayers for that person, prayers of well-being.

Prayers that your stalker gets hit by a car, run over by an 18-wheeler (by all 18 wheels), that an asteroid drops from outer space directly on his head or that God just strikes him dead with a bolt of lightning; I'm afraid do not count as praying for him or her. Those are not the type of prayers I'm talking about.

True, it is not easy for such thoughts of good for that person to cross your mind, and that's okay. It's natural, so please don't hold it against yourself.

However, deliberate desires and wishes of harm to your stalker, while they may be normal, are not good for you and they will change who you are. It is these decisively malicious thoughts that change you; they penetrate your heart and spirit.

This brief nightmare you are going through with your stalker will end. One day soon, this will be over, and you will get to go back to your life; that is what this book is all about, taking your life back. But if you allow them to change your heart and the very fabric of who you are, you can never get back to where you were. You will never be able to get your life *all* the way back. You will allow the stalker to steal something from you, to steal a part of you; a part of who and what you are.

Through all of this, you must protect your heart! Also, God instructs us that above all else, we are to first protect our hearts. We must guard your heart from that person and that evil. You cannot allow the stalker to get into your heart and make you become vengeful, bitter, and cold.

> *Guard your heart above all else, for it determines*
> *the course of your life.*
>
> ---Proverbs 4:23 (NLT)

Do not let the stalker invade your heart and therefore determine the course of your life. Please.

Pray that your stalker gets better. Pray that God help them to wake up and understand what they are doing. Pray that they get the needed help.

Pray and watch, and then, watch and pray.

OPEN UP

Once again, I know that the "O" may also be challenging for you, but you must open up and get others involved in your plight. You have to let other people know what is going on, how it started, and where it may end up.

If you wait until something huge happens, wait until that major emergency happens, then all at once you must try to explain everything that has been going on for the last several months or years, and it becomes difficult for people to grasp.

Just before I sold my home in South Carolina and closed on the little beach house near my son in Biloxi, James started to show who he really was.

James and I had been apart as of then only for about two months and I began looking forward to building a life with my son and my grandkids in Biloxi.

During this time, I continued to meet new people, many of whom became friends. One such person was a man named Marc. Marc and I dated a couple of times, though the relationship was more platonic as he was a friend and somewhat of a *listening post*. That is when I started to notice some rather strange things begin to happen.

One night Marc and I had dinner at my place and as he went to leave he found that the tires on his small pick-up truck had been slashed, all four of them! This seemed really out of the ordinary especially for the type of neighborhood it was; things like that never happened. We looked around and no other vehicles had any damage whatsoever.

We chalked it up to a case of mistaken identity. Someone must have mistaken his truck for someone with whom the tire-slasher had a grudge; this make and model was very popular.

Then, not more than a few weeks later, it happened again. This time we reported it to the police but there was not much we could tell them.

When the officer on the scene asked as subtlety as he could, uncomfortably beating around the bush, if either Marc or I had any ex-lovers out there, I wasn't sure of what to say. But I came clean and told the young officer that I knew that my ex, James, was around but I was certain that he would never do anything like this.

Yet, the police officer took James' name and description, seemingly ignoring my confidence that he would never commit such an act.

Just a few days later, after dropping me off at my place, Marc went back outside to find the windows to his truck busted out and I began to suspect that maybe James was the culprit, after all. All of this could not be a coincidence.

Marc, obviously concerned for my safety, suggested that we begin to have our lunches and dinners at his place, and we did. All was well, no slashed tires on his or my car, and no broken windows, everything was peaceful, for a little over a week.

Then one night, as it had gotten very late, I seriously began considering spending the night at Marc's place. We had not been intimate, and I wasn't planning on it that night, but I knew what could happen if I stayed over.

Then suddenly, something else happened that helped me to make up my mind. The fire alarm in Marc's apartment complex went off.

It scared the daylights out of both of us, as I am sure it did everyone in the complex.

At first, we had no idea of exactly what it was, it was just excruciatingly loud sirens that could wake the dead and caused pandemonium in the complex.

After just minutes of the chaos caused by the shrieking alarm, just about everyone in the twin buildings were gathered out in the front parking lot along with two fire trucks, a few police cars, an ambulance, and a few dozen pajama-laden, half-dressed, half-sleep residents.

It was surreal. Marc and I stood there as the kaleidoscope of flashing lights danced over everyone's faces in the dark as everyone looked for a signs of a fire.

Finding not even a burning matchstick and realizing that it was all a false alarm, Marc and I just looked at each other and thinking the same thought, I let the police know that this may be the work of James.

Believe it or not, the fire alarm went off once again at Marc's apartment just less than two weeks later. Now the police had James as a serious suspect and I was certain that this would be the end of it.

I mean, causing false fire alarms is something that the law does not take lightly. Once the police knew who he was, surely they would arrest him, scare him straight and that would be the end of it, but that is not what happened. Instead of things dying down, they intensified as I became James' direct target.

First, I began to see him slowly and methodically drive by my house in his faded, olive green Chevy Silverado. He would drive by until he was certain that I saw him and knew it was him.

One morning I returned home to find my house flooded; water all through several rooms, carpets destroyed, and lots of furniture ruined.

Upon inspection, I found that someone had broken a water pipe in the kitchen and tried to make it look like it had just busted from age. It didn't take a CSI investigator to figure out who it was. Then the so-called love-notes started.

I came home to find these crude hand-written notes, some written on paper, some on tissue, others on cardboard, scattered all over the house. They were literally everywhere; all over the counters, the television, sofa, the kitchen table, in the dog food containers, stacked up on the blades of the ceiling fan, stuffed down into my shoes, and in my dresser drawers, and even some in my nightgown and underwear.

"Love" some of the eerie little papers said. "I love you…" "You love me" he wrote on others.

That did scare me, but I think I was more shocked than unnerved, and I was mostly just plain creeped out. All I could think of was that soon, very soon, the sale on my house would be complete and I would be moving to Biloxi, MS and rid of this guy.

What proved to be one of the creepiest things ever, were signs and roses spread throughout the neighborhood. That's right, all over the entire neighborhood!

You might remember those old billboard messages they used to put up along the highways and the interstate where each huge billboard told a small part of the entire message. Like "Eat At Joes…"

The next sign might say "Great Food, Clean Restrooms…" and so on, leading to the final billboard that commanded that you "Exit Here!" In some wickedly strange way, that was what he was doing.

For instance, I found this at the entrance to my subdivision some five blocks from my house.

It's addressed to "Ruby." Ruby was James' nickname for me as it was my birthstone, but he only seemed to use it when he degenerated into Mr. Hyde. I guess it was also a way that he could make sure that I knew who it was, but would keep my neighbors in the dark because there was no one named Ruby that lived in the area.

Then there were times when James didn't care who knew who he was referring or the object of his psychotic emotions.

My God, I prayed, just a few more days and I would be gone.

Two days before my move, as I and a local handyman I had hired to repair the flood damage and to help me move were in the process of loading some things into a U-Haul Truck, James drove up and pulled right into my driveway. I called the police.

By this time, local law enforcement had several complaints from me about James, and despite his claims that he was just there to help; the police escorted him off the property and out of the area. Before they took him away, in front of the police, I demanded that he return my spare key, which he did.

Later that evening, as I sat and relaxed at the local VFW having a drink and trying to forget about the stressful day, I received a text from one of my neighbors. Connie, who lived directly behind me, said that she just saw James walking toward my house carrying a small utility bag, and I immediately called the police.

They caught James inside my house attempting to flood it again. Apparently, he had a *spare*, spare key that he claimed that I gave him, so they didn't get him on breaking and entering.

They caught him messing around with the toilet and though it was obvious what he was trying to do, it was very hard to prove, as he said he was unclogging the toilet for me.

"Lord, help me, Father;" just one more day. That day came and would prove to be one I will not soon forget.

On the morning of my last day before I closed on my house and was to leave for Biloxi, I received a text from James asking me to marry him.

Now I was sure that he was nuts. I thought that James had to be crazy and I was thinking in the clinical term. His next text said:

"I wasn't joking sweetheart. I looked it up. We can go to the courthouse show our ID's, fill out the forms and 24 hours later they issue the marriage license, we take it to the notary, return it to the court and it makes us legally married. Do up a prenuptial if you are scared I want something from you...all I want is you. Then I can go from psycho boyfriend to your psycho husband. We can make it common knowledge on your Facebook page and it will be clear to all your old flames."

As of that time, I had not had any experience or knowledge of this thing called *stalking*.

I had heard of such things and the deranged people that stalked big stars; they went after celebrities like Catherine Zeta-Jones, David Letterman, Madonna, Steven Spielberg, and Sandra Bullock.

I thought, I guess, like most of us do, that it was the fame and the fortune, in fact, it was the very celebrity of these individuals that bought out and attracted the nutcases.

As well, those people who attracted the crazies, could also afford the cost of personal bodyguards, protection, and the highest levels of security.

Of course, if you were unfortunate enough to obtain the fame before you established the fortune, things could turn out horribly different, as was the case with Christina Grimmie.

Christina Grimmie, the YouTube sensation and winner of *The Voice*, had indeed reached a level of stardom very quickly, and before she had time to build up a celebrity bank account, a deranged psychopath stalked her and killed her.

Here was James, clearly admitting that he was a psychopath, and I took him seriously. You have to take your would-be assailant seriously and you have to open up and tell people.

Investigator Jane

Corporal Jane Sloan of the Beaufort County, South Carolina Sheriff's Department was the first person to whom I really began to open up. Sure, I talked to my mother and sister, I talked to Marc and my friend Pam, but I never really got down to all of the details of what was happening until I got together with Jane.

Corporal Sloan, whom I affectionately called *my investigator*, as if she were my personal P.I., proved to be exactly who and what I needed. I had prayed for help, and the Lord answered.

As James' attacks began to go digital, he was stalking me and trying to ruin my life via the internet, I filed several internet crime reports, some which included my son and grandchildren as he was trying to hack their email accounts. This caught the attention of the South Carolina Attorney General's office and they reached out to the Beaufort County Investigative Office.

Jane was in charge of the Child Abuse Division and got my case and I can tell you that there simply was no one better to handle this than she was. Not only was Jane passionately involved and sensitive to my cause, but she was also an expert in this new thing called stalking.

The thing is that with my living in Biloxi, MS and Jane being from an investigator's office in another state, I should have never met her. James still lived in her jurisdiction, but I, the one who was bringing the charges, lived in another state.

As I mentioned, you need to first watch, and continue to pray. I did, and have no doubt that God found the exact person that I needed; the person that I could personally relate to and work with, and who knew all there was to know about the new laws involving stalking and intimate partner abuse. As He does, God just made it happen.

I opened up to Jane and told her every detail of what had been going on from the very beginning. I guess one of the reasons, in fact, the main reason I was able to open up so much to Jane, is because she almost demanded it. She constantly asked questions that forced me to dig deep and detail everything.

My relatives and friends simply did not ask the same questions that a trained investigator asked, and neither will yours. Nonetheless, you have to open up to someone and give them the details.

Keep in mind that at some point, things can come down to your word against your stalker's word.

You must realize, especially if you are a woman, that sometimes people, specifically law enforcement and courts, will not always believe you.

Often, many issues can come down to the simple fact that you told someone at some time, about what was happening. All that you may need is for someone to corroborate your story about your stalker-ex and their actions. Even though you may not have called the police, when you have someone who can attest to fact you told them the story, it adds a tremendous amount of credibility. You have to open up.

Please understand that your silence is one of your stalker's biggest assets. The stalker counts on you being silent and withdrawing into a shell. You have to open up and tell someone; join a church, get involved in ministries, contact officials in the business, like domestic coordinators and counselors, just do *something*.

I began to read everything that I could find on this stalking business and discovered that it was indeed something serious, dangerous, and real. I found that most stalkers suffered from Narcissistic Personality Disorders (NPD) and I set out to learn more about NPD and the often-resulting cycle of abuse inflicted on their victims.

Ironically, the more I learned, the dumber I acted. As I said, I'm not perfect and made huge mistakes and I pray that you do not do some of the things that I did.

The more I learned about NPD, that it was real, it was a genuine disorder, a mental condition, and it was an illness; the less I blamed James. The more I started to see him as being sick, the less I felt that his actions were his fault. How can you blame someone who is sick? Who is to blame in a case like this?

Is his mother the culprit? According to James, he grew up in poor filthy households and his mother physically abused him as a child. Could that be why as an adult, James lived in such deplorable and disgusting conditions? He was a hoarder to the point where you could not walk around in his house and you could smell the stench of cat urine throughout the place.

Could James' Narcissistic Personality Disorder just be a birth defect? Maybe that was the ultimate reason behind the irrational behavior and antisocial tendencies that led him to commit larceny while serving in the Marine Corps, which resulted in a dishonorable discharge. I began to dig deeper into James' past and upbringing.

I had maintained minimal contact with James' ex-wife, Tina and began to reach out to her as someone to open up to, and let know what was happening, as well as to pick her brain as to James' past. What Tina related to me presented a very dark, secretive, and chilling picture.

Tina told me that James had supposedly molested his sisters when they were children and had begun stealing at a very young age. Tina reported that when James and she were married, that he had numerous affairs and spent most of his time either away from their home or in seclusion when he was home.

The police also arrested him once when they finally caught him after a short, high-speed police chase for running stoplights and trespassing.

When I asked her why he had such a hard time keeping a job, Tina did not hold back. She said that he was let-go by the local fire department for bad conduct and embezzling some of the department's tools. A construction job fired him for the same reasons.

Surprisingly, James at one time, had a job as a junior high school teacher, but they fired him for exposing students to pornography.

The list of James' roller-coaster ride of a career path goes on and on with this obvious pattern of unscrupulous behavior. I learned such behavior goes hand and hand with someone with NPD, or should I say someone who *suffers* from NPD?

This person typically has a highly distorted image of him or herself and cannot take any type of criticism or rejection, which also aligns perfectly with the dictionary definition of the narcissist.

Merriam-Webster

Definition of *narcissistic*

: of, relating to, or characterized by narcissism: such as

a: extremely self-centered with an exaggerated sense of self-importance: marked by or characteristic of excessive admiration of or infatuation with oneself.

At the end of this book, you will find a Resource Directory where I give you numerous places to go to learn more on NPD. For now, let me just show you the five basic types of Narcissist.

In the article, "5 Types of Extreme Narcissists (and How to Deal With Them)" on Psychology Today's website, Joseph Burgo Ph.D., a well-known psychotherapist for over 35 years, briefly explained the five extreme narcissists types.

From PsychologyToday.com

From least to most toxic, here are five types of Extreme Narcissist you might encounter, with some advice for ways to handle them (and yourself) when you come into conflict. (Each type can, of course, be of any gender.) Bear in mind that Extreme Narcissists always need to prove that they are "winners" in comparison to other people they view as "losers," though their methods vary.

1. **Know-it-All Narcissist**

   This person is always eager to give her opinion, even when unsolicited, and believes she knows more than anyone else, no matter the topic of conversation. She likes to lecture, and she has a hard time listening because she's too busy thinking about what she wants to say next.

Coping with the Know-it-All Narcissist

If possible, ignore her "helpful" suggestions, or offer polite thanks and move on. A direct challenge will most likely lead her to escalate her efforts in order to prove herself more clever or better informed.

You might also try modeling humility and expressing a flexible point of view. Be open to her views without necessarily endorsing them. It also helps to have a sense of humor. If you're not triggered by her superior or condescending manner, you might find the Know-It-All Narcissist a bit absurd and ultimately harmless.

2. **Grandiose Narcissist**

This type more clearly demonstrates a familiar kind of narcissism we all recognize: He sees himself as more important, and more influential, than everyone else. He touts his own accomplishments, exaggerates their importance, and wants to elicit your envy or admiration. He believes he is destined for great things. When charismatic and driven, his achievements may actually match his ambition and you may find yourself drawn into an admiring orbit around him.

Coping with the Grandiose Narcissist

His assertions of superiority might make you want to stand up for yourself and compete. Don't. Any challenge will only cause him to escalate his efforts to appear superior.

On the other hand, you may find yourself drawn to a Grandiose Narcissist with charisma because you want to share in his superiority. He might strike you as a sort of celebrity, a person you'd like to submit to and serve. Be careful not to give too much: The Grandiose Narcissist won't feel grateful and will do nothing to help you unless there's something in it for him. If necessary, he will discard you without a second thought.

3. Seductive Narcissist

This person manipulates their partners by making them feel good about themselves. At first, this person will appear to admire or even idealize their target.

In return, the seductive narcissist will want to be given support and admiration. When they have no further use of the person, they give the person a cold shoulder.

Coping with the Seductive Narcissist
Don't be swayed by flattery or excessive admiration. Once you are no longer of any use to the seductive narcissist, you are no longer the center of attention to the person.

4. **Bullying Narcissist**
This person builds themselves up by humiliating other people. They may share common traits with the Grandiose or Know-it-All Narcissist, but they are more brutal about the way they assert their superiority.

They use tactics of belittling and mocking another person. When they need something from a person, they can become threatening. Bullying narcissists will make you doubt yourself and your value as a human being.

Coping with the Bullying Narcissist

Don't fight back in obvious ways to stand up for yourself. A direct challenge will only escalate their assault on your personality. In the face of their attacks, you'll need a very strong belief in your own self-worth, without having to prove it. Distance is the best remedy.

5. **Vindictive Narcissist**

This person will try to destroy their partner or any person that challenges them. They will talk negative about you to friends and family. They will attempt to get you fired from your job. If children are involved, they will turn your children against you.

Coping with the Vindictive Narcissist

Whenever possible, distance yourself before the damage to your psyche and your reputation has gone too far. This approach may require legal actions!

When I learned about the different types of disorders, I realized that I was dealing with the most toxic of them all. In James, I was dealing the Vindictive Narcissist.

When dealing with a vindictive narcissist, Dr. Burgo highly recommends that you preserve all hard evidence, keep everything, especially harmful emails, texts, and other communications. Get witness statements from any friends who may have observed unusual behaviors. This is when you need to open up, big time. If you are able, hire an attorney, and begin to document everything.

Narcissistic Injury

Another reason why you have to open up is that when dealing the narcissistic stalker, the harm to you can be deep, emotional, and psychological.

As you try to defend or fight back in any way against the narcissist, every stance you take is a direct affront to the narcissist's self-esteem and self-worth, which is the worst thing possible.

The eggshell fragile ego of the narcissistic stalker will not allow or face rejection in any shape or form and therefore they will retaliate with the most vicious and cruel avenues possible.

Your stalker will brutally attack your self-worth. He or she will try to destroy your dignity and self-respect, and do anything to bring you down, all to avoid any sense of defeat.

That is the time when you need someone who can help keep you balanced. You need people who know you and whom you have shared your plight with, who will continue to help lift you back up and keep you on your feet.

WHOLE ARMOUR OF GOD

As your life as a victim of stalking develops, you will need to protect yourself in ways other than just against the physical threats that will come your way. There is the physical, bodily harm that is imminent, and then the psychological attacks, the spiritual warfare, and today you must prepare for the internet onslaught.

Not long after my break-up with James, he demonstrated just how ruthless and ugly the internet could be when you use it as a weapon.

James had previously hacked into my emails, texts, and every form of communication that I had with everyone. While he was at it, he stumbled across conversations that I had with Giovanni.

Giovanni was an old friend I met back in 2009 while traveling to the Philippines. We met only for a brief moment at a function and that was all that came of it, besides a long-distance friendship as we just stayed in touch occasionally, mostly through Facebook. Then, in 2015, Giovanni wrote me on Facebook that he would be in North Carolina on business and Pam and I met with him for short lunch. That was it. There were never any thoughts of romance or sex or even any talk of a romantic nature between Giovanni and me. Of course, I could never convince James of this.

Six months after we split up, James sent Giovanni Facebook messages from some alternate reality. First, James told Giovanni that he and I were married, happily married at that. Then he actually began to impersonate me on Facebook. James stole my Facebook identity, created a fake Facebook account and started posting as if he were me! Then he would switch back to being himself, or rather my imaginary loving husband, and would talk about how the illicit, deceitful affair between Giovanni and me messed up his whole life.

Of course, he would also let Giovanni know that he was not the only lover I had. James would talk about my many imaginary sexual partners and he would even, man-to-man, warn Giovanni that he better be careful with me.

Yes, according to James, I ruined *his* life. That's the narcissist for you. It would be hilarious if it weren't so horribly sad.

Here is a post copied and pasted *directly* from a fake Facebook account by James: (Please note that the following is exactly as James wrote it; typos and all.

"Giovanni.. I was so glad to see you here. Here's a little walk down memory lane for you! You see I never Knew about you even though she (that's supposed to be me) was in contact with you throughout our marriage, engagement and the whole time we were dating.

My new buddy is a wizard at finding this old stuff on the internet and has shown me just what she really was doing to me.. Mike found at least two more guys that she was with while her and I were married no to mention her damn Scuba Instructor that she kicked me out for…that son of a bitch knew what he was getting into. well , never mind he will get his. We are making sure of that.

Anyway she used me and then threw me away. Ruined my life. Maybe now that I see what she truly is I can start to heal. You all have been now you know the truth."

Not only is the entire story a lie, but the real problem is that James actually believed most of it. When faced with the person who actually believes in a reality that is simply not where the rest of us live, fighting against it is like spitting into the wind. However, this is typical of the stalker personality and NPD cycle of abuse.

Narcissistic Cycle of Abuse

Christine Hammond, MS, LMHC, is a Mental Health Counselor licensed by the State of Florida with over fifteen years of experience in counseling, teaching, and ministry.

She is also author of the award-winning book, *The Exhausted Woman's Handbook.*

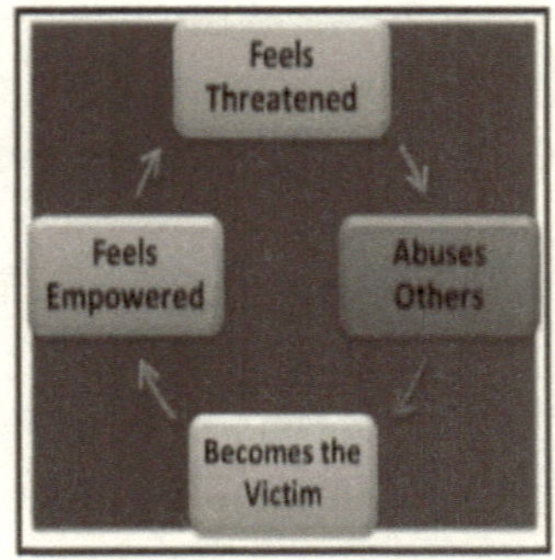

In an article on www.pro.psychcentral.com, Christine gets into that cycle of abuse.

"-----Narcissism changes the back end of the cycle because the narcissist is continuously self-centered and unwilling to admit fault. Their need to be superior, right, or in charge limits the possibility of any real reconciliation. Instead, it is frequently the abused who desperately tries for appeasement while the narcissist plays the victim. This switchback tactic emboldens the narcissist behavior, even more, further convincing them of their faultlessness. Any threat to their authority repeats the cycle."

Here are the four narcissistic cycles of abuse:

- **Feels Threatened.** An upsetting event occurs and the narcissist feels threatened. It could be the rejection of sex, disapproval at work, embarrassment in a social setting, jealousy of other's success, or feelings of abandonment, neglect, or disrespect. The abused, aware of the potential threat, becomes nervous. They know something is about to happen and begin to walk on eggshells around the narcissist. Most narcissists repeatedly get upset over the same underlying issues whether the issue is real or imagined. They also tend to obsess over the threat over and over.

- **Abuses Others.** The narcissist engages in some sort of abusive behavior. The abuse can be physical, mental, verbal, sexual, financial, spiritual or emotional. The abuse is customized to intimidate the abused in an area of weakness especially if that area is one of strength for the narcissist. The abuse can last for a few short minutes or as long as several hours. Sometimes a combination of two types of abuse is used. For instance, a narcissist may begin with verbal belittling to wear out the abused. Followed by a projection of their lying about an event onto the abused. Finally, tired of the assault, the abused defensively fights back.

- **Becomes the Victim.** This is when the switchback occurs. The narcissist uses the abused behavior as further evidence that they are the ones being abused. The narcissist believes their twisted victimization by bringing up past defensive behaviors that the abused has done as if the abused initiated the abuse. Because the abused has feelings of remorse and guilt, they accept this warped perception and try to rescue the narcissist. This might include giving into what the narcissist wants, accepting unnecessary responsibility, placating the narcissist to keep the peace, and agreeing to the narcissistic lies.

- **Feels Empowered.** Once the abused have given in or up, the narcissist feels empowered. This is all the justification the narcissist needs to demonstrate their rightness or superiority. The abused has unknowingly fed the narcissistic ego and only to make it stronger and bolder than before. But every narcissist has an Achilles heel and the power they feel now will only last till the next threat to their ego appears.

By all accounts of all therapists and studies, this person is extremely volatile and dangerous. In this battle, you have to be armed to the teeth; not only with your pals, Mr. Smith and Mrs. Wesson, but you need the put on the Whole Armour of God.

Whole Armour of God

Whoa! Now this is being prepared for battle.

Let me tell you a little bit about the Armour of God, and if you happen to be someone who does not believe as I do, please stay tuned.

I will explain exactly how understanding the *concept* of putting on the *Whole Armour of God*, just may save your life; not just spiritually, or metaphorically, but literally and physically.

What I mean is that if you do not believe in the Bible, keep reading because we will look at every part of this from a nonspiritual point of view as well.

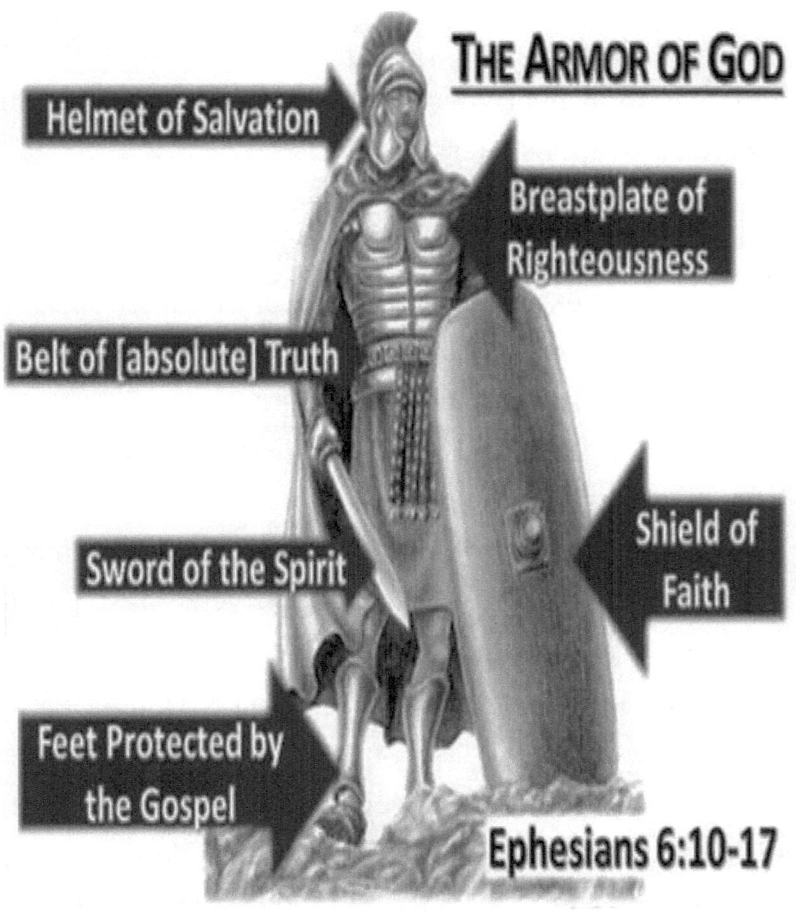

"The Whole Amour of God" is a powerful phrase that we find in the Bible in the book of Ephesians chapter 6, verses 10-18.

The Bible, and as I have repeated, often talks about how we, Christians, are in a perpetual battle against the enemy, that is the devil, satan.

As I have mentioned earlier, this enemy is not your common everyday foe and does not fight with everyday weapons. Remember…

"For we wrestle not against flesh and blood, but against principalities, against powers, against the rulers of the darkness of this world, against spiritual wickedness in high places."

---Ephesians 6:12 (KJV)

While the Bible is symbolic in some places, in my opinion you can consider the above verse as a literal truth and take it seriously.

While your stalker may use his verbal abuse and physical attacks with fists, sticks and knifes, you have to understand that your defense with the same fist, stick and knifes will not be enough. Your stalker, whether they know it or not, has the backing of the true enemy behind him.

While your attacker may come at you brandishing a fist made of flesh and blood, you can bet that the power and lethality behind those bare knuckles is a host of wickedness in high places.

I don't say this to alarm you and the Bible did not either. The Bible simply made it clear as to how you need to protect yourself against this enemy. The Word of God gives us specific instructions on how to go into battle against our enemy.

Just before, and immediately after the above verse, God talks about the Armour of God. He then explains what it is; that is, what every piece of the amor is and why it is important.

Here is Ephesians 6:10-18 in the King James Version. Then, I will break it down a bit in the Amplified version, and then I'll approach this for those who are not of the Christian faith.

Again, if you are not into this, bear with me. As I go over each part of the Amor of God, I will look at each one, first from the spiritual point of few, but then I will also talk about each piece of Armour from a purely nonspiritual point of view as well.

So please bear with me because no matter what you believe, you will find this very helpful.

Ephesians 6:10-18 King James Version (KJV)

The Armour of God

[10] *Finally, my brethren, be strong in the Lord, and in the power of his might.*

[11] *Put on the whole armour of God, that ye may be able to stand against the wiles of the devil.*

[12] *For we wrestle not against flesh and blood, but against principalities, against powers, against the rulers of the darkness of this world, against spiritual wickedness in high places.*

[13] *Wherefore take unto you the whole armour of God, that ye may be able to withstand in the evil day, and having done all, to stand.*

[14] *Stand therefore, having your loins girt about with truth, and having on the breastplate of righteousness;*

[15] *And your feet shod with the preparation of the gospel of peace;*

[16] *Above all, taking the shield of faith, wherewith ye shall be able to quench all the fiery darts of the wicked.*

¹⁷ And take the helmet of salvation, and the sword of the Spirit, which is the word of God:

¹⁸ Praying always with all prayer and supplication in the Spirit,

and watching thereunto with all perseverance and supplication for all saints;

So we are to put on this whole Armour of God, why?

"…that ye may be able to stand against the wiles of the devil…"

And that Armour consists of six important pieces:

1. The Belt of Truth: *"having your loins girt about with truth,"*

2. The Breastplate of Righteousness: *"and having on the breastplate of righteousness;"*

3. Shoes of the Gospel: *"And your feet shod with the preparation of the gospel of peace…"*

4. The Shield of Faith: *"Above all, taking the shield of faith…"*

5. The Helmet of Salvation: *"take the helmet of salvation…"*

6. The Sword of the Spirit: *and the sword of the Spirit, which is the word of God*

That just about explains it all for me! But let's break it down in a more up to date language version.

Ephesians 6:10-18 Amplified Bible (AMP)

The Armour of God

[10] *In conclusion, be strong in the Lord [draw your strength from Him and be empowered through your union with Him] and in the power of His [boundless] might.*

[11] *Put on the full Armour of God [for His precepts are like the splendid Armour of a heavily-armed soldier], so that you may be able to [successfully] stand up against all the schemes and the strategies and the deceits of the devil.*

12 *For our struggle is not against flesh and blood [contending only with physical opponents], but against the rulers, against the powers, against the world forces of this [present] darkness, against the spiritual forces of wickedness in the heavenly (supernatural) places*

13 *Therefore, put on the complete Armour of God, so that you will be able to [successfully] resist and stand your ground in the evil day [of danger], and having done everything [that the crisis demands], to stand firm [in your place, fully prepared, immovable, victorious].*

14 *So stand firm and hold your ground, having [a]tightened the wide band of truth (personal integrity, moral courage) around your waist and having put on the breastplate of righteousness (an upright heart),*

15 *and having [b]strapped on your feet the gospel of peace in preparation [to face the enemy with firm-footed stability and the readiness produced by the good news].*

16 *Above all, lift up the [protective] [c]shield of faith with which you can extinguish all the flaming arrows of the evil one.*

¹⁷ And take the helmet of salvation, and the sword of the Spirit, which is the Word of God.

¹⁸ With all prayer and petition pray [with specific requests] at all times [on every occasion and in every season] in the Spirit, and with this in view, stay alert with all perseverance and petition [interceding in prayer] for all [d]God's people.

Wow! Now that should be clear.

The Armour of God

First, you must be strong in the Lord and the power of *His* might. You want literally to draw your strength from Him and through your relationship with Him.

"…be strong in the Lord [draw your strength from Him and be empowered through your union with Him] and in the power of His [boundless] might."

1. The Belt of Truth

"…like the splendid Armour of a heavily-armed soldier], so that you may be able to [successfully] stand up against all the schemes and the strategies and the deceits of the devil."

Please stop and just think for a moment. Is it not, *"schemes and strategies and deceits,"* that you deal with in your relationship with your narcissistic intimate partner?

Remember, this person will come at you with everything; every single little slimy trick and lie available. He will boldly claim to be the innocent party and blame you for running his life. The culprit will accuse you or being the attacker and, as you read earlier in my case, even pretend to *be* you.

Your criminal assailant will launch and spin so many lies and different stories that you will find yourself questioning what is actually true and what is not.

James had manufactured the fantasy of he and I being husband and wife and at one time having a great loving relationship. Then he spun it so many times and in such detail that every once in a while, I had to stop and ask myself if it had really happened.

People who live in such an alternate reality and preach it over and over again, will have others around them, who listen to them, believing in that reality as much as they do.

Listen, there is only one way you can deal with this onslaught of fabrications and deceptions and that is for you to be firmly grounded and rooted in the truth. You must have on the *Belt of Truth.*

Now, to most Christians and I, the Belt of Truth means the truth of the Word of God and the truth *in* the Word of God. That is the truth in Christ, who *is* the truth.

"Jesus saith unto him, I am the way, the truth, and the life: no man cometh unto the Father, but by me."

---John 14:6 (KJV)

We know that Jesus Christ is the truth and also the Word.

"And the Word was made flesh, and dwelt among us, (and we beheld his glory, the glory as of the only begotten of the Father,) full of grace and truth."

---John 1:14 (KJV)

Jesus, the Christ, is the Truth and He is the Word. So we should have our waist, which is our very body, wrapped by the Truth of the Word (Christ).

Now, I don't know about you, but I would say that is a great first step in going into battle.

So that is my spiritual view of the Belt of Truth, however, let's talk about its importance from a nonspiritual, worldly point of view.

You still need to have yourself firmly planted in the truth as in the facts, as in reality, as in historical accuracy.

When it comes down to it, in a court case, your nutcase will stand there looking just as cool and calm or pitiful as ever, and will start telling 27 different variations of the truth, and will do it without the slightest hiccup or mistake.

Then when it's your turn, you start fumbling and mumbling and, "Oh, ah, ah, no...that's not what I meant..." and "Oh, yeah, I forgot that..."

That just does not look good.

The last thing you need is to be in court or in some other critical situation and look like you don't know whether you are coming or going, and that is exactly what a tornado of lies can do to you if you are not girded in the belt of truth.

2. The Breastplate of Righteousness

Righteousness, in the most basic of terms, means goodness, innocence, honesty, justice, purity and all that is right.

Of course, with those stipulations, most people cannot accuse any human of being righteous. The Bible clearly states that,

"For all have sinned, and come short of the glory of God..."
---Romans 3:23 (KJV)

Therefore, no human has any justification to claim righteousness or to have the ability to wear anything that is righteous.

However, the truth is that it is through *justification,* the stage of the salvation process that wipes out your sins, everyone saved by the blood of Jesus Christ, is made righteous.

Most Christians understand that Jesus died for their sins on the cross at Calvary over 2,000 years ago. However, what many do not realize or understand is that His death did so much more.

The death of Jesus and the resurrection of the Christ, did surely absolve our sins and the sins of the whole world.

However, His death was also a *substitutional atonement.* Christ made an exchange, in that He substituted Himself for us, for you. He changed places with you.

At the time of His death, Jesus took your sins, but He also gave you *His* righteousness! Jesus gave you His glory. He gave you His power. He gave you His purity and goodness.

Now, a breastplate covers your vital organs including your heart; your *righteous* heart, which you must always protect and guard with everything you've got.

"Keep thy heart with all diligence; for out of it, are the issues of life."

---Proverbs 4:23 (KJV)

The Breastplate of Righteousness protects you from the devil's accusations and allegations and guards your heart. You need to wear the Breastplate of Righteousness, the glorious righteousness of Christ, to protect your righteousness heart.

For the nonbeliever, let's take a look at it from the nonspiritual viewpoint.

While it may be true that you are an innocent victim, you may have to convince many people who don't not know you personally, of this truth, and believe me; it is not as simple or as easy as you may think.

You must be innocent.   Remember, James accused me of having illicit and sexual affairs with dozens of men.

I can assure you that if one, just one of those accusations had proven to be right, or even look to be the truth ...that would have been it. Case closed.

Even with dozens of things against him, all that it would have taken is just one single bad thing against me, and I would have become the slut who ruined his life.

Your accuser will accuse you of everything under the sun. Do not let there be anything true. You have to be right and innocent and show it. You cannot let the accuser have anything of substance that shows you doing wrong. Don't lie, don't cheat and no matter how hard it is, do not retaliate in kind. This is no time to fight fire with fire. You have to be as right as rain. Put on the Breastplate of Truth.

3. The Shoes of the Gospel

Going into any battle, a solder will have comfortable, well-fitting, and protective footwear. For the believer, it cannot be any different with you and your battle. Your feet, your very walk, must be secured in Christ.

The Bible says that we that have accepted Christ should also *walk in Him.* We must walk as He did.

"…whoever says he lives in Christ [that is, whoever says he has accepted Him as God and Savior] ought [as a moral obligation] to walk and conduct himself just as He walked and conducted Himself."

---1 John 2:6 (AMP)

The enemy will put more obstacles in your path than you can imagine and remember the devil is using things that we can't use, like the minds and imaginations of other people. The enemy will put other people in your path; people you may not even know who can act as *agents* for the enemy. These things will pop up in your path and try to derail everything that you try to do.

Police and people who are supposed to protect you will act as if you are crazy and don't believe a word you say. Doctors will doubt you and write things in your medical records that can come back and haunt you later. The devil's influence is wide-ranging and deep.

The only way you can circumvent this is to have the Gospel of Jesus Christ as your foundation. You need to have the Gospel control your every step.

For the nonbeliever, you know what it's like when you hear yourself saying something like "What in the world was wrong with that person?" Or, "Why did that nurse treat me like *I* was the bad guy?" I am sure you know what I mean.

Whether you believe these things are spiritually orchestrated or not, you have to admit that often, inexplicable things happen that make is seem like there is some kind of conspiracy out to get you and bring you down. You are not crazy or paranoid; it will seem like that sometimes.

At these times, you had better know your path; your *exact* direction and be able to stay on it. You need to know where you are going and what your final goals and outcomes are. You have to be on *sure footing* or you will be tripped up.

4. The Shield of Faith

The Bible says *"...above all...take the shield of faith..."*

The great and humble apostle Paul, who penned the Book of Ephesians while in prison, tells us the most important piece of the Armour is the shield of faith. He also tells us exactly why the shield is so important. Paul continues to inform us of the harmful, even deadly weapons from which it protects us.

"Above all, taking the shield of faith, wherewith ye shall be able to quench all the fiery darts of the wicked."

---Ephesians 6:16 (KJV)

What exactly are the *fiery darts* the enemy will launch at you? Fiery darts represent a host of spiritual munitions, the most devastating of which are *doubt* and *fear*.

When doubt begins to overwhelm you, and I do mean *when*, you need to be able to lean on your faith. There will be times when you feel that it's all over; you will feel like all of your work and efforts are useless and that no matter what, it is all hopeless. You will feel that all of your struggles are in vain and futile, and will want to give up and give in to your stalker.

At times, you may want to just to give up, and yes, it can even get to the point where some victims turn to suicide believing that is the only solution.

The American Psychological Association says that the percentage of victims of domestic violence and intimate partner abuse that choose to kill themselves can be as high as twenty-three percent.

When doubt begins to creep in, the only effective weapon is your faith. You may think that you do not have enough faith, or you do not have strong enough faith. However, God gave each of us the measure of faith; that is, *the same measure* of faith.

"For I say, through the grace given unto me, to every man that is among you, not to think of himself more highly than he ought to think; but to think soberly, according as God hath dealt to every man the measure of faith."

---Romans 12:3 (KJV)

The Bibles says "the" measure of faith, not "a" measure of faith. A measure of faith can easily mean that you have a measure; I have a different measure and a measure over here, a measure there and so on.

However, *the* measure clearly indicates that everyone has the same measure, the same amount of faith. We also know that the amount of faith you need to work the greatest miracles in the world is not very much.

"And Jesus said unto them, Because of your unbelief: for verily I say unto you, If ye have faith as a grain of mustard

seed, ye shall say unto this mountain, Remove hence to yonder place; and it shall remove; and nothing shall be impossible unto you."

--Matthew 17:20 (KJV)

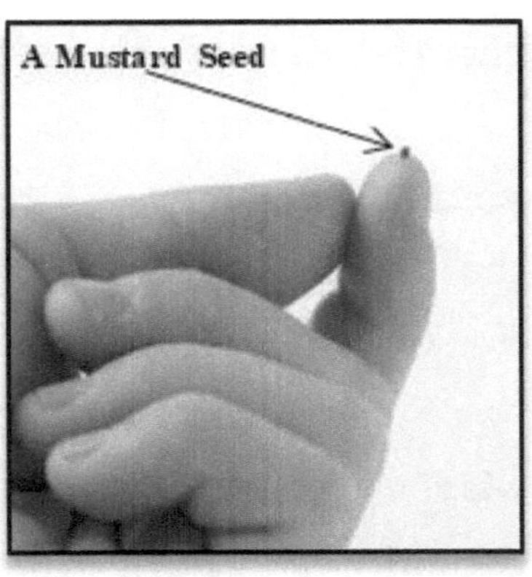

That's it, that's all the faith you need to move a mountain. I love it that the Lord uses a mustard seed as the example. I mean, have you ever seen a mustard seed?

When doubt and fear begin to mount, you can find yourself not able to sleep, rest, or relax. Overpowering anxiety and feelings of terror and apprehension of an impending catastrophe for reasons you will not be able to explain to anyone may haunt you.

Your only defense in this *battle of the mind* is your faith. Yes, above all else, take with you the shield of faith.

For the nonbeliever, you have to have a solid rock to lean on and depend on.

You need something that is greater than you that can lift you up and strengthen you when you are weak and experiencing fear and doubt.

These moments can be tremendously powerful and completely overwhelming and if not properly checked, they can be devastating and life shattering.

You must have a pillar of strength and power in your life that you can turn to in these times. Maybe that is a group of people, friends, or supporters. I do not know who it is for you.

However, I implore you, not to take this lightly. Maybe you might want to try faith and Jesus. It certainly can't hurt. If that is a thought, hang on and I will show you exactly how to bring Christ into your life with one short prayer.

5. The Helmet of Salvation

Speaking of a battle of the mind, you will need the Helmet of Salvation to guard against satan's literal mind-blowing deceptions of the truth and the basis of your very salvation.

The key, rather the glue, to all of the above is the fact that you, as a Christian, have been saved and born again. Should the enemy be able to shake up your confidence in your own salvation, everything falls apart.

You have to be absolutely sure of who you are and whose you are. You might wonder how can you be so sure? How can you know for a fact that you are saved and still going to Heaven?

I know many Christians believe that you can lose your salvation and that every time you commit a sin you lose your right standing with God. Therefore, you have to be saved over and over again and at no time can you be certain of your status.

I feel so sad for those who live this way. Living in this condition, there is no way to have any sense of security in your salvation because you are not the one who is keeping score. It is a horrible way to live, in constant fear and doubt, scared nearly every day of your life.

However, I can assure you that the most High God, the one and only Creator of all things, is not some guy on the street or some slipshod business that will give you something and then take it back.

Everything that God does is eternal. Again, I won't turn this into a Bible lesson, so I will keep in short, as short as God does in the Bible.

God settled this question and all other questions in one single sentence in the Holy Bible. In one short verse, the Lord detailed what it is all about, what _everything_ is all about.

In that one verse, God tells why He created us, why He is saving us, why He did everything, and He explains how long it all lasts. It is all in one short, very familiar verse.

"For God so loved the world, that he gave his only begotten Son, that whosoever believeth in him should not perish, but have everlasting life."

---John 3:16 (KJV)

I won't get into breaking this down too much, but you really ought to study this verse one day, and I mean study it. It summarizes the entire Bible.

John 3:16 makes it clear on what it takes to be saved…

"…whosoever believeth in him…"

That's it. Done. *Whosoever;* which means everyone and anyone, who just believes in Him, Jesus, will not perish, period.

There is no fine print. There are no other pre- or post-requisites. Once you believe in Him, that's it…saved.

It continues and nails the question with which so many people have a problem.

"...should not perish, but have everlasting life."

Let me ask you something "How long is everlasting?" I am pretty sure that everlasting means something that lasts forever, right?

Think about it, how can you have something that is everlasting only for a short time?

Once you believe in Him, you have <u>*everlasting life.*</u> If you ever *had* everlasting life, then you still have it, or it was not everlasting in the first place. Does that make sense?

If you had everlasting life, but do not have it any longer, then it was never everlasting to begin with.

God clearly said that once you believe in Him, that you are saved and that it lasts forever. God does not add at the end of the verse, "...until you commit a sin..."

Now, either you believe what He said, you believe that God's Word is truth, or you believe that John 3:16 is wrong and God lied. Which is it?

You would have to believe that either God flat out lied or He failed to tell us everything and left out pertinent information. Of course, we all know that a lie of omission is still a lie.

God said that your salvation is assured and guaranteed. You can live boldly, not proud; but confident and faithful in Him.

However, the devil will attack your mind with the thought that you are not who you think you are. The enemy will attack your mind and constantly accuse you of being a lowly, horrible sinner that God has cast aside.

These thoughts will come at you right in the middle, while you are in battle against your narcissistic nutcase, and it can mess you up. Do not let it. Just shout aloud…

"Get thee behind me satan, in the name of Jesus!"

For the unbeliever, you too need to have something or someone who can help you know that you are who you know you are and that you are not losing your grip on reality.

Seeing a therapist is not anti-Christian and sometimes therapy can help a lot. You may need someone who can assure you that you are in your right mind, when your victimizer comes at you wielding insanity weapons.

6. Sword of the Spirit

Finally, in your outfit for battle, is the Sword of the Spirit. While a sword can be used for defense, actually it is the only part of the Armour essentially offensive, because every other piece is defensive in nature.

The Sword of the Spirit does as it says in the Bible; it is the Word of God. The Word is powerful and shaper than any two-edge sword.

"For the word of God is quick, and powerful, and sharper than any two-edged sword, piercing even to the dividing asunder of soul and spirit, and of the joints and marrow, and is a discerner of the thoughts and intents of the heart."

---Hebrews 4:12 (KJV)

Let me give you that verse in the Amplified version, also.

"For the word of God is living and active and full of power [making it operative, energizing, and effective]. It is sharper than any two-edge sword, penetrating as far as the division of the soul and spirit [the completeness of a person],

*and of both joints and marrow [the deepest parts of our
nature], exposing and judging the very thoughts
and intentions of the heart."*

---Hebrews 4:12 (AMP)

Remember, you can't use only human weapons against your stalker. True, it is not a bad idea to have some ready, locked, and loaded as I did. However, you will need more than these types of weapons.

The Sword of the Spirit, which is the Word of God will cut through the gibberish and the mirage and help you see clearly. The sword protects and destroys at the same time.

Remember how at one time I felt sorry for James? I started to feel like I could help him. He was sick, and he needed my help. The man was ill and he loved me, and was pleading for my help. How could I be so cruel as to abandon him at that point in his life?

There will come the times when your stalker will plead, cry, and beg that you just understand that he or she loves you.

If you were married, didn't you vow to love whether for richer or poorer and in sickness and health? Well, this is sickness.

This will be an incredibly powerful draw on you, especially if at one time you were in love with the individual. Now that they have become sick, what do you do?

The Word is your only sense of clarity to discern the truth. Is it possible that your ex is telling the truth?

Yes, it is. In fact, most of the time that person *is* telling that truth in that he believes what he is saying.

But *telling the truth* and *the truth* are two different things and you need to be able to discern the difference. You need the Word of God that will cut through the muck and mire like a two-edged sword.

For me, the Word of God helped me see through James' lies and destroy his ploys at the same time.

For the unbeliever, you too need to know beyond any shadow of a doubt when your stalker is telling the truth, as in being honest in that they believe what they are saying, and when he or she is telling what is actually true.

Perhaps you have a mastermind group of people who you regularly confide in and keep up to date with everything that is happening.

You will have to keep in mind though, that these people will be biased in one way or the other. Some will want you two to get back together and see almost anything that your ex does as good thing.

While others may want you to just kill him, figuratively or actually, and move on.

This is also a critical reason to open up and get people involved in what is happing from the beginning. It is the only way for those people to have any context of what is going on.

How do you put on the Whole Armour of God?

The way to put on the Whole Armour of God is to recognize and live in the consciousness and full awareness that you have the righteousness of God bestowed on you by our Lord and Savior, Jesus Christ and that you are an heir to the Kingdom of Heaven!

How do you become an heir to the Kingdom? Just get saved. Want to do that right now? Okay, got a minute?

Remember, the Lord said, *whosever asks...will be saved*, and he is a God of His Word!

Simply pray this short prayer...

"Dear God, I want to be a part of your family. You said in Your Word that if I acknowledge that You raised Jesus from

the dead, and that I accept Him as my Lord and Savior, I would be saved.

So God, I now say that I believe You raised Jesus from the dead and that He is alive and well. I accept Him now as my personal Lord and Savior. I accept my salvation from sin right now.

I am now saved. Jesus is my Lord. Jesus is my Savior. Thank you, Father God, for forgiving me, saving me, and giving me eternal life with You. Amen!"

That's it! If you said that prayer, you are now saved. You are saved and nothing can change that.

Listen; all of the other crap and ridiculous hurdles and hoops are all nothing but man-made, devil-assisted complications and distractions due to our inability to understand the absolute unconditional love of God. Amen!

EXONERATE

As I mentioned earlier, this step certainly is not going to be easy, at least it surely wasn't easy for me. However, I can assure you that no matter what, you are going to have to get to and past this step. You will have to exonerate everyone involved; you will have to forgive.

Yes, I am talking about you forgiving the person who has tried to make your life a living hell, the person who has assaulted you, the person who may have physically hurt or maimed you or tried to kill you.

Yes, you will need to forgive that person. If you think that is going to be difficult, hold on because it gets harder.

You are going to have to forgive yourself. Your first thought might be "What? I didn't do anything wrong, I'm the victim."

True.   However, during your ordeal, or depending on where you are in the process of getting your power back, you will have to deal with the places you went; the depths that you sunk to or were prepared to reach.

You will have to deal with the fact that before all of this began, you were a mild-mannered, God-fearing, peace-loving woman who would not harm a fly. Then, almost overnight, you turned into a raging, bloodthirsty maniac ready to kill and you had the lethal firepower to do it. I hope that you never got to or will ever get to that point.

Yet, there are things that you did, will do, or even just thought about doing, that you will have to deal with. I had to come to terms with the fact that on more than a few occasions, I was bunkered down in my house, ready, willing, and fully able to blow James' head clean off.

Now of course, this was a purely defensive stance and there was nothing wrong with it, as it was only in the event of saving my own life. Still, this will weigh on your conscious when this is all over and you are back to your normal self.

You will have to face the horrible thoughts that you had about your stalker. All of those times that you honestly wished, and even prayed, that a huge meteorite would fall from space directly on his head.

Even now, I am sure that there are some who are reading this and thinking that you would much rather kill your ex-intimate partner than forgive them.

At some point, you are going to have to forgive yourself for those types of feelings, as just as they may have been.

You will have to forgive your assailant, you will have to forgive yourself, and you will need to exonerate all of those people who you felt were somehow in-league with your stalker.

There are many people who, often unwittingly, aided the criminal in their efforts to harm you. In addition, there are the people who stopped you or made it outrageously difficult for you to get the protection or the information you needed. Then there are those people who just wouldn't listen to you or believe you when you cried out for help.

I am talking about those two police officers who came to your house and didn't believe a word you said only because your stalker didn't leave a single clue. Or the idiot on the phone, who told you that you could not take out a restraining order. Or even that woman at the library who gave you such a hard time about using the computer because you were too afraid to log on using your real name.

For some of us, we hide these people and what they have done, or what we think or imagine they have done, deep down at a near subconscious level in an attempt to forget all about the incidents. Then for others, these people are front and center, on a long list of people to *pay back*.

It's like the list "The Bride" (played by Uma Thurman), had of people she would *take care of* leading up to when she would finally *Kill Bill*, in Quentin Tarantino's movie of the same name.

That is not you, at least not now, or not anymore. You will have to reconcile this in your own mind, heart and spirit.

There are the many spiritual and Godly reasons that you need to do this, as we all know that God told us to forgive, and that we should love our enemies and so forth.

However, I am not referring to the spiritual or moral reasons that you need to forgive right now. I am talking about the plain ordinary physical, temporal, reasons why if you do not completely exonerate your stalker, you can never be free.

The only way to get your power back is to forgive that person who put you through hell.

This is a fact...

If you do not forgive, it is impossible to get your power back and you will never be free.

Please allow me to explain exactly why that is.

James' Plan of Reconciliation

Not long after I moved to Mississippi and started to feel a sense of peace, my spirit went into combat mode. For some reason, I began to carry my little .380 and started to walk and move with unrelenting vigilance.

I began to question my own sanity. Was this what I had become? Walking around in a dark clouded state of paranoia, ready to turn and shoot the first person who tapped me the shoulder to ask what time it was.

It had been over a month and no trouble, no problems, no James. I should thank God and relax, I thought.

Finally, on the morning of May 3, 2016, a bright and sunny Tuesday, as I began to leave the house for a brisk morning run, I stopped. I thought, do I really need to carry a gun to take a leisurely jog around the block, seriously? I put the pistol down on the little table near the door.

I opened the door to see exactly why my spirit had been on alert. James had littered my door stoop with pictures of him and me.

In the middle of the photos, he left a vase of roses and a note. On the paper, he had written "Love Me," in serval different languages.

The sight stunned me and pushed me back into the door as if I had been hit with a bolt of lightning.

The roses stared at me. They just sat there, and I could swear they were looking at me, watching me, smiling at me in some sort of a creepy way.

Each picture jumped up at me and I could hear the faint sound of that screeching music from the shower scene from Alfred Hitchcock's "Psycho" echoing all around me.

James was back. He's back.

My stomach sank as I shut the door and grabbed my .380 and raced to the back of the house to make sure all of the doors and windows were secured and locked. I exchanged the .380 for the .357 Magnum and checked the ammo in the other guns I had hidden around the house. I was terrified.

I sat down on the floor in the living room, my arms around my knees, .357 in hand, and sat there for what could have been hours.

"When will this ever end?" I thought. "This will never end. It is never going to end."

I began to think about killing James, for real. I don't mean killing him in an act of self-defense or while he was breaking into my house. No. I seriously contemplated killing him in a most offensive way.

I thought that maybe it was time completely to turn the tables. I would track *him* down, go to *his* place, crawl in a window, and wake him up by sticking my magnum in his mouth. Then just as he was awake enough to know that it was me standing over him, I'd pull the trigger.

Who was I kidding? I could never do anything that. Or could I? Actually, I wasn't sure. How else would I ever have peace? Was that the only way? If so, it was not only logical, it was smart.

It would be a few days before I could shake those feelings of murder and get my head back on straight.

I prayed. I prayed more.

I would later need to forgive myself for allowing him to get me to such a point.

You may look back and find that you had things cross your mind and many that lingered there in which you will need to forgive yourself.

Later, the same day that James left the shrine on my doorstep; my son John received an email from James. How he got John's email, I don't know. The email was sent to John but was meant for me.

The email message talked about arranging a meeting between James and me and he demanded that I reply to the attached agreement. The whole thing clearly demonstrated a deranged mind.

In the email, James threatened,

"If I have not heard back from one of you by 8PM tonight then I will head back to Beaufort SC in the morning and assume you wish for me to pursue legal recourse..."

What?   What in the world was this maniac talking about?   I started not to even open the attachment, but thought that at least it may give me some idea of what he was up to.

James titled the letter his "Reconciliation Plan" and it was purely psychotic.

His plan included sections such as

1. Purpose
2. Term Violations
3. Forgiveness
4. Communication
5. Visits
6. Proximity
7. Relationships
8. Social Media
9. Conclusion and
10. Meeting

Clearly, he had become an attorney in his own warped mind. Here is an excerpt of this very disturbed so-called plan written by James:

"Violations:

Makayla-Should Makayla violate the plan during the term James may move forward with legal action to have their common law marriage declared in the courts and divorce in accordance with the laws of SC.

James-Should James violate the plan during the term Makayla may choose to dissolve the plan at that time and James agrees to not move forward with any legal action or further pursue any relationship between the parties.

Social Media:

Transparency is key to good relationships. Any use of any social media will be accompanied with an invitation for the opposing member to join said site. Wherever possible a relationship between parties shall be revealed and shared on sites.

Makayla will activate her Facebook account, unblock, and friend James and list him in some sort of relationship status. No postings to any social media regarding the opposite party shall be derogatory, abusive or in any way violate the decency of that party. Use of multiple accounts for whatever reason must be disclosed to the opposing party."

It went on like this for all of those so-called sections, ending with a place for me to sign and date it. I thought that it was hilarious that he could actually believe that I, or anyone on earth, would sign such a thing. My son John though, did not take it lightly and insisted that I come and stay with him for a few days, to which I agreed.

The next day we confirmed John's feelings as the police caught James near my house with tools to break in. They called me and I met up with an Officer Morgan, and since they didn't have enough to arrest him, I made a citizen's arrest.

Forgive him? This man put me through a literal hell for years, and I'm just supposed to forgive him?

That's how I felt. I just forgive him, and he gets away with everything that he did? Or perhaps he does finally go to jail; still that can't pay me back for what he did. Believe me; I know how you may feel.

Yet, I still say that until you let go and let God handle it, you will never be free.

You Remain Imprisoned

You must understand that when you forgive the one who harmed you, you do it not for *that* person.

I might even say that when you forgive that person, don't' even do it for God. When you forgive, you forgive for yourself.

When you *do not* forgive, why is it? What is it that makes some of us stubbornly to refuse to forgive?

It is usually because you seek revenge or some other form of apology or recompense from the assailant.

The problem with this is that while you wait for that compensation from your stalker, you are forever tied to, and indebted to, him or her. As long as that person refuses to come to you and apologize, beg your forgiveness, or admit that they were wrong, and did horrible things to you, you are stuck.

Who do you think has the power in this situation? *You* surely do not. When you fail to forgive, you relinquish all the power and all the control to the stalker.

Years after the nightmares are over, and the nutcase has gone on to torture some other poor soul, and has completely forgotten about, you will still be stuck, wallowing in the fact that your ex still owes you something.

That person still owes you something and you will never be complete, you will never be whole until you get it. That is a truly horrible place to be and a worse way to live.

What if your stalker dies, then what? Would that free you?

In the event of that person's death, you will still not have received your payment. Your goal, your wish, or rather your vividly imagined dream, might be for the person to call you while on his deathbed, and have his last dying words be what you so longed to hear.

Or you could dream that even though you were not there to witness it, that she did finally relent, repent and admitted her wrong doing. However, the truth is that is not going to happen and now you will be stuck forever.

To take your power back, start by taking back the power of imprisonment. Start by forgiving that person or you will never be free, but tethered to the person for the rest of your life.

That image reminds me of a short story that I think clearly illustrates this point.

Girl and the Bumble Bee

On a beautiful summer day, a woman strolls leisurely through the neighborhood park when she comes across a young girl sitting on a bench.

At first, the woman just nods a polite "Hello" to the young lady, but then she notices that the girl seemed to be grimacing in pain.

She stopped and moved closer to find out that surely enough, the girl was in agony; her eyes nearly shut and holding back tears, sweat beading up on her forehead and she was squirming in the seat.

"Oh my!" The concerned woman said. "Dear, what's wrong? What is it?"

"Aghhh..." The girl squeezed out. "I'm, I'm fine."

"I beg to differ, young lady." The woman insisted. "What are you sitting on?"

The young lass gave in. "I'm sitting on a big bumble bee that stung me. Aghhh! "

The woman's mouth dropped open in a gasp, but she said nothing.

"He stung me right in my rear end," The girl continued. "The stinger is still in me and still attached to the bee!"

"What?" The woman screamed. "My God child, get up off it!"

"Nope!" The girl said defiantly. "No way, owww! I am going to stay right here"

"But why?" asked the woman.

Then the bumblebee girl explained her reasoning.

"That bee stung me and I'm not going to let him get away with it!

So, I am paying him back!"

Ironically, this is what it is like when you hold on to those things that your stalker has done to you.

Of course, all the girl had to do was get up.

First, the stinger would likely dislodge from her rear and come out from the bee as well, probably killing the bee in the process, and the whole thing would be over.

Even if the stinger did not come loose, still the situation would be over one way or the other.

By continuing to sit on the bee to exact revenge, the girl is the one who suffers the most and she cannot move or go on with her life. She is trapped. She is imprisoned just as you are until you forgive your stalker.

Now I will be the first to admit that forgiving is much easier said than done. So, just how do you get yourself to forgive this person? How can you get past minor lip service and actually forgive that person in your heart, for real?

Frankly, I don't believe that we *can* truly forgive. I do not believe that you or I can. However, like it says clearly in Philippians 4:13

"I can do all things through Christ which strengtheneth me."

We all know this verse and many of us are quick to quote it. But let me draw your attention to one word in the scripture. It is *"through."*

It says "I can do all things *through* Christ..."

It does not say I can do all things with the help of Christ.

It does not say I can do all things by praying to Christ.

It says you can do all things by operating through, Him. That is to work inside of Him as He is inside of you. Christ living in you, you then have the power as He is already in you. Concentrate on Him and do as He did.

Then, also like Christ, pray to the Father, which we also do *through* Christ. That's why we always, say, "...in the name of Jesus I pray..." We pray *through* Him.

One thing to do to help you get to the point of true forgiveness is to pray for your stalker. Depending on where you are in the process, that thought may have made you nauseous.

Yet, praying for him or her will really help. At first, you will know that your prayers are nothing more than lip service and that you don't really mean a word that you are saying. But that will change; just keep doing it.

I started praying for James a long time ago, before I had ever thought about writing this book. In fact, I began routinely praying for him after he tried to have me arrested for trying to kill him.

No, this was not a time that I actually did try to kill him, this was some crazy thing he concocted in his head.

Arsenic & Old Lace

I often made these delicious little Columbian cheese arepas for the family. Everyone loved them and I took great pride in making these arepas that are similar to small meat pies or sandwiches. I had made some in April 2016 and after the family ate, we had several left over. Trying to be nice, I dropped the leftover arepas at James' dive shop. I expected nothing in return, except maybe a small thank you as at this time, we were merely estranged. However, what I got was far more than I could have ever imagined.

Apparently, James saved the arepas for several months and in August of that year, he wrote a letter to the Beaufort Sherriff's Department claiming that I tried to poison him and he presented my little cheese snacks as evidence!

This was simply unbelievable. I had considered just describing the letter he wrote to the Sherriff, but I didn't think I could correctly capture the mind of this man, so I thought it best just to let you read this.

What follows is the actual letter. Of course, if you get to the point where you feel you have read enough of this man's thinking, just fast forward to page 149.

8/29/2016

"As I am writing this I am wondering if I am completely crazy. Unfortunately, enough adds up that I am afraid and feel I need to put this down so that if something happens there will be a record that will cause someone to look into it.

I have a suspicion that I have been poisoned by my ex-wife Makayla. I believe she used some sort of heavy metal and that I am now suffering the effects of that poisoning. Makayla is a nurse wellness coach and holds a doctorate of holistic medicine.

I know she kept a kit of holistic medicines in the bathroom at our residence. She also maintained a friendship with the owner of a holistic medicine and herb supplier in Savannah, GA. I believe it is called Ye Olde Herb Shop. While looking into my symptoms and my suspicions I discovered that several toxic materials are used in holistic medicine such as a form of mercury called cinnabar.

As I look back at our relationship there are some things that now seem odd when viewed with my suspicion of poisoning. We were "married" on June 6th of 2014. Makayla was still technically married to her ex-husband.

The story I was told was that he was an alcoholic and that he had abandoned her. Nobody including his family knew where he was or how to contact him and so he could not be served for divorce.

I was very much in love with Makayla and we had no plans to have any children so it didn't seem important that we could not get a marriage license.

We held the wedding ceremony to show our commitment to each other and for appearances for our families. I considered her my wife and believed her to consider me as her husband.

Shortly after we got married Makayla insisted that we take out life insurance policies. As my line of work, scuba diving, involves some risks this seemed to make sense to me at the time.

She worked out the details set up the policies, physicals and arranged payments. I was told there would be a $20,000 policy on each of us payable to the other in event of our deaths. I later found that she never took out a policy on herself and that she holds a $50,000 policy on me. "

(Oh my goodness. I really could not believe he would say such things, as not one bit of it is true.)

"When I asked her about this she said it didn't matter as she couldn't afford to keep it up and had dropped the policy shortly after talking it out.... But somehow I don't believe that. I know she maintained a life insurance policy on her ex-husband throughout our relationship.

For a while Makayla insisted that I take vitamins. Makayla made breakfast every morning and would set out my vitamins with breakfast. At first that was no big deal and I figured they were probably good for me she is a wellness nurse after all... after a few months though something changed in them. I started to get nauseous after taking them sometimes vomiting within a few hours.

I tested this by not taking them and I would be fine when I went back to taking them again sure enough I would get sick again. I started pocketing the vitamins at breakfast and throwing them out later.

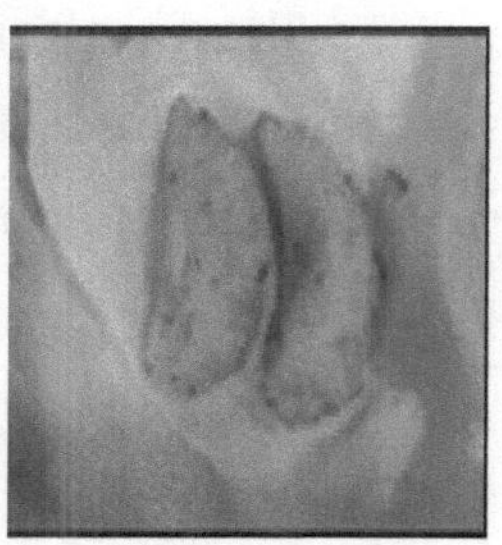

It wasn't worth arguing with Makayla about them and I just let her think I was taking them.

Eventually, when she was out of town on a trip one time I threw the bottle of them out and she never said anything about it and they never reappeared. She also made coffee for me every day that I took with me to work.

Sometime I want to say around October of 2015 something in the coffee changed. I'm not sure if it was a flavor or a texture but something didn't seem appealing to me.

I assumed that Makayla had changed brands of coffee or creamer. I loved the fact that my wonderful wife cared enough to get up early and make coffee just for me every day and I didn't want to disappoint her and say anything was wrong with it.

I've never been a big coffee drinker anyway so most of the time I would take a sip or two and then dump the rest out. Occasionally, on a cold morning I would drink the whole thing, but that was rare.

On April 23rd 2016 Makayla brought some cheese arepas to me at the shop. I didn't think anything of it at the time but this was odd. She sent food with me regularly but had not brought me food since before we were married.

It wasn't unusual for us to meet up at a restaurant or for me to go home to get something she made for lunch but she never went out of her way to bring me something at the shop.

On the 23rd I had a group going out for a dive. She arrived and dropped off 3 or 4 fresh arepas right before the group arrived... I had time to eat one or two before I put the rest away in the refrigerator. Somehow, the leftovers got pushed to the back of the refrigerator and I forgot about them. I was cleaning out the refrigerator last week and found the two remaining arepas. At that point something seemed to click and I started looking into the symptoms I have been experiencing since the beginning of May 2016 and came to the suspicion that I had been poisoned.

Our last day living together as husband and wife was April 25th.
On Aril 26th as she was moving the last of her possessions out of the house she forced a fight between us on the lawn that drew the attention of the neighbors and of course the police.

The story she told made it seem like we had never been more then boyfriend and girlfriend, and that I had not been living with her for some time.   She then moved to Biloxi, MS and cut off all communication. I believed she knew that if she sent no word at all, that eventually I would follow and try to open communication with her.

On May 3rd I did go to Biloxi and left roses and a note at her doorstep. I believe this was all planned so that she could distance herself from me as I went through the symptoms that she knew would follow. I believe this situation was also to put stress on me so that those symptoms could be blamed on that stress and would either be overlooked or at least not to be associated with her. She was also well aware that I am not the type to go to a doctor for just about anything and that I currently have no health insurance and could not afford to go to a doctor even if I wanted to.

Picture taken 2016 New Year's Eve

Seven months later I started losing weight almost immediately by May 5th I was down 14 pounds and by May 14th I was down 17 pounds from a weigh in on April 16th. On June 17th I was down a total of 23 pounds and as of this writing I am down 26 pounds. I now weigh less then I did

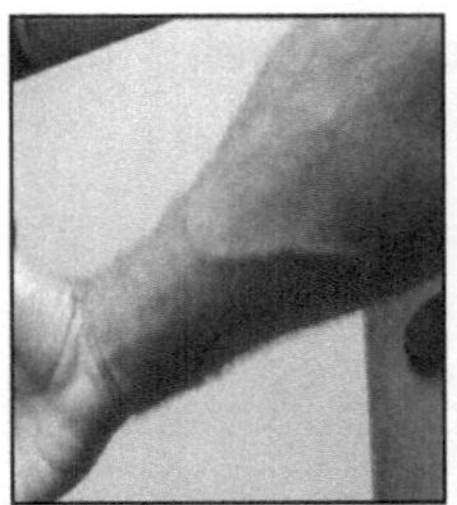

when I got out of the Marine Corps 20 years ago. My blood Pressure in contrast has gone up. Prior to May 1st it averaged 110 over 60. It is now averaging 125 over 78.

During this period I have also gone through a deep and dark depression. Makayla's leaving at the end of April, an accident on my dive boat that resulted in a death on May 7th, and the passing of my grandfather July 23rd, may have contributed to this but I do not believe that the severity and endurance of this depression fits with my nature or background.

Insomnia is also a constant problem since May. I rarely sleep more than 4 hours at a time now and often go days without sleep. Prior to May 1st I never had a problem sleeping and rarely got less than 8 hours.

I began noticing a sudden hair loss in May as well. Large amounts of hair began to show up in my comb and blotchy bald areas appeared on my head, chest, genital area, and legs. There is no history of major hair loss in my family much less one that has been as rapid as this has been."

(He continues like this talking about strange rashes, showing pictures of his arms and legs, a deteriorating gum disease and everything from dizzy spells to debilitating brain damage.)

"Last week I was hit with the sensation of a sharp object being driven between my ribs on my left side below my arm. It is sudden and sharp and doesn't seem to be attached to any kind of repeatable movement or pressure on the location. There is no rash, bruise or other indication or source on the skin in the area. I had a similar sensation in the back of my right leg just above the knee and as I was putting my weight on that leg at the time it caused me to fall.

I also seem to have regular headaches. I have had migraines occasionally in the past but these seem to be far more frequent compared to what I have ever experienced before.

My hands and occasionally my feet have been going numb it doesn't seem to be tied to anything I can pin down just suddenly get the pins and needles feeling. Sometime there is a dull ache and other times they shake.

It has been pointed out to me that I may be having some memory loss. In teaching scuba classes I seem to lose my place and stammer over words and stories that I have told for 20 years of teaching. I don't know how to test this but it is very worrisome to me at this point.

I understand that heavy metal poisoning has no real cure or treatment and can take months to run its course. I hope that should anything happen to me that I should be checked for some sort of poisoning along with the leftover arepas that are currently stored in my refrigerator."

Projection in its Purest Form

The narcissist is the king of projection. That is taking everything that they themselves are, or are doing, and projecting on others.

In their July 2018 blog *"5 Ways Narcissists Project and Attack You"* by Darius Cikanavicius, PsychCentral.com sums it up this way:

"Most narcissists generally lack self-awareness. Indeed, their sense of self-esteem and self-worth depends on how others perceive them, and they tend to deny flaws in themselves and blame others for their own shortcomings, mistakes, and misfortunes. This is called projection, and people with narcissistic tendencies are projection-heavy individuals."

The blog goes on and mentions that when the narcissist constantly accuses you of being a cheating spouse; you can bet it is he or she, doing the cheating.

In the case with James, the projectionism was clear. While he was accusing me of trying to kill him, he was constantly trying to kill me as well as to disturb, disrupt, or even kill my family.

Targeting My Family

By November 2016, I started receiving some very disturbing messages from my mother and sister back in Beaufort.

One day they opened the door to find beer bottles sitting up on the fence near the front gate. This may have not been too creepy, except for the fact that they were, of course, James' brand of beer.

A bunch of dead roses in the front of the house followed the beer bottles a few days later. Then, my sister stepped out of the front door only to find dozens of nails scattered all over the stoop. All we could do was to keep a detailed record of everything that was going on.

Those little scare tactics seemed to slack off after my youngest son Anthony, flew to Savannah, GA, rented a car and went to visit my mother.

After taking a long survey of the house, he set up three surveillance cameras around the perimeter of the house, and for a brief moment, there was peace.

I received a text from my sister saying that something was wrong with the brakes on her car. Alarmed, I called and she went on to tell me that she now had to press her brakes to the floor to get them to work.

She carefully drove the couple of miles to her mechanic's shop at about 15 miles per hour and barley made it.

It only took two minutes for the auto mechanic to confirm that someone had cut her brake line. It was only the little bit of fluid that was already in the system that gave her any pressure at all.

This maniac was really trying to kill us, and I found out that he would spare no expense in carrying out his goals.

The Cruise

Right after I sold my home, I decided to splurge. Some of my girlfriends and I had formed a group that we called "It's a Girls Thing."

We would get together and go out to clubs, dinner, bowling, and so forth. This time, however, we decided to take a cruise. We hooked up with a travel agent and arranged a cruise to Puerto Rico and Caribbean Islands in December.

The months leading up to the trip were calm and peaceful since James had apparently decided to leave us alone for a while. The agent circulated a monthly newsletter to all of us with news, ideas, and constantly updated information on the upcoming trip. I began to look forward to the journey more and more, as it also would help me escape the often nightmare of reality, if only for a little while.

In one of the newsletters, the agent suggested that we all wear the same color shirts to make it easy to locate one another and we unanimously choose orange, as the excitement became a fever and the day arrived.

We met up in Miami and traveled to the Carnival Cruise Lines Terminal together. I almost couldn't believe it was happening. Life was going on, continuing on, after James.

As we stood in the terminal amidst the hundreds or thousands of excited cruise goers, the Lord spoke to me and told me to look around.

I had no idea of why God was telling me to look around the room, but obediently I turned and slowly began to scan the large area.

Then, through a crowd of people, my heart stopped in the middle of a beat, my body froze, and my knees weakened, as my eyes centered on James.

I couldn't believe it, but there he was, in the terminal, boarding the same cruise. My mind raced, dazed, and confused. How? Could it be a coincidence? How could he be here?

Then I noticed that he also had on an orange shirt! Oh my God, he must know everything, I thought. Of course, he had probably hacked my email or someone's in the group, and had all the information about the cruise; he had the whole itinerary and bought a ticket.

It all started to make sense. That is why he had been so quiet in the months leading up to the cruise. He didn't want me to be on guard or watching for him; he wanted me to start to forget about him. He knew what he was doing.

Then, as he was looking down at the papers in his hand, he turned and saw me, our eyes locked. He showed no expression, he just turned and looked away. It was a wide-awake nightmare.

Why the orange shirt? I guess he had planned to get me alone and push me overboard and if anyone saw from a distance, it might look like someone in our group. I don't know, but it was crazy enough for him.

I jumped out of the check-in line and immediately told, or rather warned everyone in my group that my stalker was on board the ship. They all knew the story behind James.

(Once again, this is proof of why you have to open up and let people know. Imagine if I had just brought up James for the first time right then? I tell my girlfriends that this guy is my ex and he bought a cruise ticket and got on board just to terrorize me. Not only that, but if anyone of my group had confronted James, he would have acted like he didn't even know me and he's a good actor. They would have thought I was crazy. I know I keep hitting you over the head with this, but it is crucial.)

I ran over to security who called in the Port of Authority Police. I was shaking and crying as I desperately searched for a copy of my restraining order. I wasn't even sure if I had it; why would I need it? I was trying to explain the whole story and the history, but I imagine it all sounded like gibberish between frantic breathing and sobbing. However, the PA officer had no interest in arresting James, stating he would not have the authority.

A couple of my closest friends and I went to the captain of the ship, The Carnival Glory, Captain Nikkos, and as calmly as humanly possible, explained the situation and how James was dangerous.

To my surprise, although I could not produce a restraining order, Captain Nikkos believed us. I am sure the two thousand prayers that *It's a Girls Thing* sent up, had something to do with it.

The captain gave James a choice; he could use his ticket to get on another ship heading somewhere else or he could go home. Less than an hour later, security escorted James off the ship; his new destination, Mexico.

Forgive This?

Of course, you, just like I have, would have to think, just how in the world can anyone forgive all of this? How am I supposed to let it go? This man literally terrorized me for years and tried to kill me and members of my family. Sure, everyone says that you have to forgive, but the question is how?

To forgive, to exonerate, you must give it to God. I mean this literally, not just spiritually. I believe that we, that is, humans, do not truly have the capacity to forgive; it is not in our nature. We automatically, inherently move to get back, to strike back, and to seek revenge.

When someone hits you, before even thinking about it, your automatic stance is to hit them back. It seems intrinsic; hardwired in our DNA.

To get to the point where you can honestly exonerate your stalker, you will need to let go of it, admit that you cannot forgive on your own and ask God to take over. You need to be honest with God and let Him know that you *want* to forgive and just as He said, He will make it so.

Remember, you can do all things, *through* Christ; that includes forgiving. Do this through our Lord.

Pray *for* Him

I believe the defining moment for me, the time when I knew that I had truly forgiven James down in my heart, is when I was able to pray for him. Or should I say when I was able to pray for him and mean it.

Pray for your stalker, and that of course, means to pray *good* prayers. As I mentioned before, praying that harm comes to that person doesn't count.

When you start praying for the person who terrorized and harmed you, at first, you will know that it is merely lip service. But continue and let the Lord know that you know where you are and the condition of your heart. He knows anyway. Then, you will begin to heal. You will begin to let it go and that is when you will begin to become free.

I was eventually, able to forgive James. I forgave James, forgave myself for all the thoughts and even some of the things I did. I forgave the Port Authority officer not arresting James. I forgave myself for what I thought about that officer when he refused to arrest James.

I forgave other police officers for their intentional or unintentional actions or inaction in my case. I forgave court clerks, lawyers and judges and everyone I could think of for whom I, at some point, had some real bad feelings.

Then I was made free.

"And ye shall know the truth,
and the truth shall make you free."

---John 8:32 (KJV)

The verse says that the truth shall *make* you free. That is "make" you free, not "set" you free. Several English versions translate this verse with the word *set,* instead of make, as it is in the Original King James.

So what is the big difference between to *make* you free or to *set* you free? Without getting into a long sermon, very briefly, this is the difference.

First, the truth is not the simple truth as in a statement that is not a lie. The truth, as in relation to this scripture, is Christ Himself.

Remember, *He* is the truth, He is *"...the way, the truth, and the life..."* – John 14:6.

Jesus was saying to everyone as they continued in His Word, that they will come to know *Him.*

Anyway, to be *set* free means to be set apart, or set away from; set or separated from something. So, if you are inside a prison and I set you free, it means that I have taken you out of the prison and set you apart from it. I have *set* you free.

Whatever the thing is that is holding you or imprisoning you, if you are set away from it, you have been set free. To be set free clearly indicates a prison or confinement that is physical and tangible.

However, what about a prison, confinement, or something that imprisons you that is not physical? What about something that is spiritually, mentally, psychologically?

The fact is that you cannot be set apart from something that is not physical. You cannot be set free from an intangible prison.

You cannot be set free from hate or fear. You cannot be set free from memories that haunt you. You cannot be set free from the horrors that your stalker put you through. For this, you have to be *made* free.

To be made free is to be created, constructed, completed, built, shaped, fashioned, and formed free. Free from anything. This is how a prisoner serving a life sentence can be free without getting out of the jail cell.

When you are *made* free, you are free indeed!

RENEW, REFRESH AND REGAIN CONTROL

Yes, believe it or not, this too shall pass. Whatever it is that you are going through, no matter how difficult, dangerous, and devastating it is, no matter what horrible, hateful or hideous things that your stalker has done, the day will come when it is over.

When you keep your eyes and keep your focus on the prize, the finale, the end game, that is Christ; you will prevail.

Keep your mind focused above the fray and stay on Him, and He will keep you in perfect peace. He told us so...

"You will keep in perfect peace
all who trust in you,
all whose thoughts are fixed on you!"

---Isaiah 26:3 (NLT)

Remember your power and remember your P.O.W.E.R.

P.O.W.E.R.

P = Pray and Watch

O = Open Up

W = Whole Amour of God

E = Exonerate

R = Renew, Refresh and Regain Control

After, or even well before, you get through the other steps it will be time, as it was for me, for the R; time for you to Renew, Refresh and Regain Control.

Renew

When you are born again, that is when you are saved, should you believe as I do, God *regenerates* your spirit. God actually rebirths your spirit, which is the essence of what you are and you become a new person, or more accurately; a new creature.

"Therefore if any man be in Christ, he is a new creature: old things are passed away; behold, all things are become new."

---2 Corinthians 5:17 (KJV)

Being born again is simply the best analogy I can think of to what you need to do at this point. As with when you are born again, you do not lose your memory and forget everything that has happened to you.

God does not wipe your mind clean, nor does He miraculously get rid of your scars. When born again, you still have the same physical body and the same mind complete with all the memories, the good as well as the horrendous.

However, a transformation does take place. After rebirth, a new set of principles now guide your body and your mind as your new spirit now guides you.

This is exactly what you need to do here. As we talked about in the last chapter, Exonerate, this is not going to be easy, and nearly every fiber of your being will want to hold on to some part of what happened.

A part of you will want to get even in some way; it is how we are wired and why you need to renew yourself. Otherwise, you will be forever tethered to your stalker.

You need to step out of your past life and into a new one. You don't forget what happened, but you do turn the page.

Refresh

Shake it off and refresh your computer screen; the computer screen of your life. Turn the page and move on. Take one step, that's all, just one step. Then take another. Then another. Soon you will be running and jumping and doing everything that you used to do before the sick events began.

It all ends with you believing that the nightmare will end, and that soon, the morning will come.

I actually started writing this book in February 2018. That is right in the middle of everything that was going on between James and I.

I started writing this book while I was living the nightmare with my crazy and dangerous stalker, and I can tell you that even then, I *knew* that the book would have a happy ending where I was the victor not the victim. I knew; or rather let me say that God assured me, that I would not be a victim, but a victor.

I knew that I would not only be a survivor, but I would be a *thriver*!

I had no idea *when* the story would end, nor did I know what the ending would be. Yet, I did know that it would indeed end and that it would be a positive ending.

Some of the events in this book happened while I was actually writing the book! Some of the events, I guess you could say, were written *live*.

When I began, it was just to keep record and carefully document everything that was going on, as I advise you to do. Then, when I noticed that the devil stepped in and tried to stop me in every way that he could, I knew that there had to be more to my writing everything down than just as a record. I knew that my writing had a much greater purpose.

That's when the Lord gave me the thought that other people could benefit by what was happening to me, and what I, through Him, was going to do about it.

Of course, there were times when I thought that it was all over; times when I felt like just giving in, when I was terrified. There have been or will probably be times, when you will feel the same, but just hold on and remember that the morning will come.

Diver Down

It's 2:24 p.m., Saturday, May 7, 2016. Even though the clouds hung low and overcast the entire Beaufort County area, it was a fairly nice day, thus far. That is, until I received the following message from James.

"We just had a drowning on the boat...I know you don't want to hear from me but well if I ever needed you it is now!"

Not knowing exactly what in the world this meant, I did not respond. By early 2016, James had already proven that he would do anything to get my attention and lying and making up crazy stories was one of the least of those things.

A few hours later, I got an email from one of James' friends, or rather, one of his cronies, also talking about an accident where a diver had died.

The next day a newspaper article confirmed the fact that a 57-year old man, an apparently very experienced diver, had drowned on a diving trip hosted by James' business.

I cannot say exactly what happened and it smelled like negligence, but I don't believe any charges were ever bought against his dive shop.

However, a couple of tidbits came to light; most notably that James did not have a business license or a diving license, not even for a hobby. Further, he lacked the licensing even to operate a charter boat.

Negligence? Maybe.

Was my stalker capable of murder? Of course he was. I knew that first-hand, as he had tried to kill me. It was one great big mess, a huge mess that I had to, just like you will, turn the page on and take a step forward.

In fact, I once heard someone say that you need to take your *mess* and make it your *message*. I did exactly that and so can you.

Make Your Mess Your Message

In making my mess become my message I started at my church, Faith Tabernacle, where Rev. James L. Black is pastor.

Together, the pastor and numerous church members and I spearheaded a community awareness program on ending domestic violence and we took to the streets.

Members of the church, their kids and friends would go out and hold up signs on the busy intersection of Pass and Popps Ferry Roads. Several drivers honked horns in support of our cause, while others quickly glanced and drove by us. I wondered how many of those were actually victims or knew victims like me.

The move was not so much to generate money or anything, just awareness of this crime that so often exists hidden or camouflaged in our communities.

The church hosted a community awareness breakfast meeting; it was sort of a Town Hall Meeting and invited our local police department representatives to educate us on how we can better partner with law enforcement.

Pastor Black selected one other church member and I to share our stories. Although, public speaking was not something new to me, this would be the first time I would share my story, my personal testimony of pain and fear, with an audience.

As I stared out into the audience and began to speak, I watched for their reactions to various examples of cyber stalking and relentless harassment. At first, I thought that maybe I was overreacting; maybe my situation was not as bad as I thought, because the audience seemed to remain stoic.

As I went on, I got into exactly how I felt and expressed the onslaught and constant anxiety of a coming storm of battery, the ever-present threat of physical violence, and what it felt like to have every aspect of my life and privacy violated by this man.

At one point, my voice became shaky and emotional, and my eyes glossed over with water, but no tears fell. Still the response was silence.

Then as I looked a little closer, I could see that the silence from the community residents in attendance was not from indifference. They were not hearing my story through shallow ears. They were stunned.

As I began to look into the eyes of the audience, I could see that they were in near shock, eyes wide open and mouths hanging agape.

"Yes." I thought. "They get it. They understand."

After the breakfast meeting, members of the Women's Empowerment Center asked me to join the center and help champion their cause as a member of the Board, to which I enthusiastically accepted.

I felt empowered.

I *was* empowered.

I felt good.

I felt renewed.

By the grace and mercy of God, I had truly begun to regain control.

I became a passionate *prayer warrior* of the church, sharing authentic empathy for those in troubled situations with no apparent way out. I also was getting involved in the critical cause of *preventing* domestic and intimate partner abuse.

Helping those who have suffered abuse is one thing, but stopping it from happing in the first place is a far better objective.

In addition to writing this book, I knew that I had a responsibility to help educate the public. I had a duty to inform as many people as I could reach about the perils of stalking and what they can do if they find themselves in the predicament.

In January 2017, I wrote and submitted *A Letter to the Editor* to several newspapers in Mississippi and South Carolina, many of which published the letter.

Below is the essence of that important letter I submitted.

Letter to the Editor

"The purpose of this letter is to educate the readers on the growing problem of stalking and to help others who are going through this same ordeal, which I refer to "guerilla warfare". Here are three simple offensive-defensive tactics that will help.

Lesson #1: Learn the stalker's tactics! Stalkers do the following:

- Make unwanted phone calls, including hang ups
- Leave unwanted messages and emails
- Show up places where and when they are not wanted
- Watch, follow, or spy on a victim with a device, camera or GPS
- Leave strange or threatening items in and around your home or place of employment
- Sneak or break into the victim's home or car in such a way to let the victim know it was the stalker
- Leave unwanted or unrequested items such as flowers and cards

When these types of things begin to happen, you must understand that they are not coincidences and they are not friendly gestures.

Lesson #2: Take pictures and videos. Save all documentation in chronological order.

When you see the things listed above happen, take care to document them. You will need the evidence when you go to court. It is also a good idea to spreadsheet or log noting the exact time and date of each incident.

Lesson #3: Contact the authorities, domestic abuse centers, hotlines, family members and friends.

Stalking and harassment is a serious matter. Do not think the stalker will not harm you or even kill you. Remember that one day it will be over, it will end. "

This Too Shall Pass

On June 29, 2018, just after the last time police arrested James, investigators Jane Sloan and Brandon Disbrow interrogated James.

Of course, James denied everything, from mailing me the dozens of cards, hacking my emails and other cyber accounts, phone tampering, harassing my family, cutting my sister's brake line. Everything.

Jane asked James why he had targeted Allan, the guy I was dating. James had hacked all of Allan's personal online accounts and even though it was clearly obvious, James denied doing anything wrong.

If you have not figured it out by now, narcissists are prolific liars. They will lie no matter what the evidence and proof that they are lying. They will look you square in the face and swear to you that the sky is orange while standing outside under the clear blue sky.

Below is a text James sent to Allan. He actually sent Allan a Bible verse from Proverbs. Believe it or not, in James' deranged mind he believed communicating with Allan through these verses would somehow change things or make Allan run away.

He would quote Proverbs 6:25 to Allan constantly. What does that proverb say?

*"Do not lust in your heart after her beauty
or let her captivate you with her eyes."*

James had also signed me up on the mailing lists of practically every state park in the country. I have no idea what insane motivation he could have had for doing this, but every day, my mailbox was flooded with brochures and state park information to the tune of over fifty pounds of mail.

When Jane questioned James about it, she brought the tub of mail I had collected, and James' jaw visibly dropped open in the courtroom. At that point, he shut down and asked for an attorney.

Case Evidence

James had a handwritten note *in case of an emergency* in his wallet, with my name as the point of contact and even listed my phone number and Biloxi, MS address. He also left a handwritten will behind, in which I was listed as the beneficiary.

At his dive shop, Jane found piles of garbage and it was an uninhabitable filthy pigsty and hoarder's paradise. There was an old, wrought iron makeshift cot where he slept, surrounded by a moat of pictures of me.

James also left pads of paper around with the passwords to my email and online accounts, in addition to all sorts of information on my ex-husband.

In the woods, where James took off running before the police apprehended him, he had stashed the envelopes and stamp pads he used to send me greeting cards, and the weapons he hid, in a Rubbermaid container; *my* Rubbermaid container.

The main prize however, was in his truck, where Jane found the latex gloves and actual knives he used to cut my sister's brake line.

Stalker James would end up in the South Carolina State Penitentiary in Columbia, SC.

During James' bond hearing I was able to read my Victim's Statement to the court.

Here is a copy of my victim statement. The bold section kept me focused while I patiently sat in court.

*I am BRAVE! I am a VICTIM who has
stood up to Stalking!*

2 Corinthians 12:9

***"My grace is sufficient for you, for my power is made
perfect in weakness."***

***Therefore, I will boast all the more gladly about my
weakness, so that Christ's power may rest on me.***

VICTIM STATEMENT READ OUT LOUD IN COURT:
1. INTRODUCTION
    - Your honor, my name is Dr. Makayla Anderson
    - I am a registered nurse and United States Veteran
    - 6 years ago, I met the defendant at his scuba shop. He is a former intimate partner. (I regret the day I ever met him)

I am here today to share with the court the full impact of his devious crime, but most all the reasons why his bond should not be reduced and reasons why he should not be released.

2. HISTORY
Three years ago, after the relationship ended, my nightmare began. By April 27, 2016, multiple police calls had been made. For safety reasons, I fled Beaufort and moved to Biloxi, MS in attempts to start a new life and open my wellness practice.

Four days later, the defendant crossed 4 state lines. While I was sleeping, he trespassed on my property and left a very disturbing shrine. Red roses, poster signs and several hundred note cards with the words "I love you" in many different languages.

Later that afternoon, he returned. Climbed over the fence and attempted to enter my home. Within minutes, a police officer identified the defendant running away from my home. James Oden was apprehended, detained and later released.

The defendant returned to Beaufort and attacked me on a different level, he chose to cyberstalk. He compromised and infiltrated all aspects of my personal life. He hacked my emails, utility accounts, Amazon, Facebook, bank accounts and violated HIPPA by gaining access to my patients' personal information.

Without my authorization, he uploaded videos and pictures of me on different social media sites in an attempt to ridicule and discredit me. I did not sleep or eat for many nights thinking I was going to lose my job. At this point, I was withdrawn and detached from my family and friends.

By December, a group of friends and I decided to go on a cruise. The ticket was purchased online months prior. After James Oden hacked my emails he learned about the details of the cruise and purchased the same trip, on December 10, 2016.

I was standing at the Miami terminal and noticed the defendant in line ready to board the ship. My heart sunk and I could not believe my eyes. I was fearful knowing the defendant would attempt to board the ship and push me overboard. I contacted Port Authority; the defendant was escorted away from the terminal and was not allowed to board the ship. A police report was filed and Biloxi court violated him on the order of protection.

The defendant returned to Beaufort, this time he chose soft targets. My 76 yr. old mother, who is frail and has health issues. My sister, who is a grade-school teacher. Your honor, by now, I reached the darkest moment in my life. The people I most love were now at risk. The defendant threw carpenter nails in my family's driveway. He stalked them on a daily basis. My sister's brake line was severed, which nearly cost her life. The unimaginable was taking place.

By January 2017, James Oden was arrested for harassment 1st degree here in Beaufort, SC. While out on bond and wearing an ankle monitor, he continued to harass. He was ordered not to be anywhere close to my family. But yet, on an ankle monitor he followed my sister and shoved a Valentine's card in her trunk. Of course, the defendant denied it. But the ankle monitor 'pinged' him at the exact location where my sister had parked her car.

The defendant pled guilty to harassment 1st degree and was given a 3-year probation. By January 2018, James Oden chose a new target, my fiancé, Harrison County Sherriff deputy Allan Cramer. The defendant included my children as well. Repeated the same offenses, hacking, prank calls and infiltrating every aspect of their lives. Evidently, there are no boundaries for James Oden, as he will attack every person in my circle, friends and family members.

3. CLOSING

By June, 2018, I was relieved to hear that the defendant was apprehended for violating his probation. But what is most disturbing are the weapons he was in possession of. Since the defendant's incarceration, I have had nothing but PEACE.

I can come to Beaufort and visit my family and friends without having to look over my shoulder every minute. I can drive my car knowing that it hasn't been tampered with or tires slashed or brake lines cut.

Your honor, last night I crossed 4 states lines to say, "This man is very dangerous and is a flight risk." His pattern and behavior repeats itself over and over. Other judges, and his own attorneys, have warned him to stay away and stop his devious crimes.

I fear for my life and every person who is dear to me, my family, friends and fiancé.

Thank you your honor.

DENIED!

After my statement, the judge denied James bond reduction and held it at $250,000. That's the type of bail people get for murder, which I thought was appropriate.

Whenever I was in Beaufort SC, I would park my car outside of the jail, sit quietly, think, and pray. I'd gaze at the barricaded exits and entrances, huge fences topped with razor-sharp barbed wire and the guards in high towers with machine guns and I pray that God will forgive James for his actions and one day wake him up.

However, it was not over. How I so desperately wanted to believe it was all over, I knew that it was not. I knew that it was not finished.

I knew that, in fact, depending on what happened at his trial, this nightmare could just be sliding horribly into its second terrifying act.

In December 2018, they extradited James back to the Beaufort County local jail where he was to face more charges of stalking.

Again, his public defender and I, and the district's attorney of course, waged war as the bail amount to be set for this criminal. Again, they pleaded for a drastic reduction and again I was there to plead to the judge to not allow this maniac to roam the streets and once again...Denied! James was to remain in custody until his trial; today.

Wednesday, January 22, 2020, 9:30 A.M.
THE LEGAL BATTLEFIELD

The Trial

This is it. The 14th Judicial Circuit Court Courtroom #3, Second Floor.

This is how it ends. At first, I felt nervous, frightened, and apprehensive and justifiably so. I mean, my Lord, should the court go easy on this man or even let him off the hook prematurely, or God forbid, they find some ridiculous technicality to let him go free, my world would come crashing down yet again.

Then, God tapped me on my shoulder and admonished me for having such thoughts and immediately I dismissed them. God was right, of course, and the Holy Spirit washed me once again in the blood of Jesus Christ, and I smiled.

I felt strong, I felt at peace. I felt the power of God in me and through me. I felt the power. I had the power, I had the control, and I had the authority to quickly remedy any situation that could come out of this.

I looked over at Donna and she grasped my hand as the bailiff instructed, "All rise!"

The next several minutes went by like a light flashing on and off, as one moment I was there, in the court and fully lucid. The next moment I was in a trance or asleep. It was as if my mind tuned out things that I did not need to hear.

A few minutes passed and then I heard, "In the case of The State of South Carolina versus James Oden..."

Then the bailiff was announcing, "Bring in the jury!"

The jury just strolled into the courtroom from a side door right beside where they would sit. They consisted of eight women and four men, which I thought was appropriate.

My mind started to wonder how the wolf (his lawyer) would use those fake phone call conversations and to set it up to make me look like the criminal.

I shivered and Donna huddled closer.

No!

"Satan get behind me in the mighty name of Jesus!"

I shouted in my heart and immediately looked around to see if I had said that aloud. Noticing everyone still looking forward, I realized, to my relief that I did not.

Again, I yelled the affirmation in my mind and centered my thoughts on the fact that it doesn't matter what they do; it doesn't matter what tricks they pull, nothing, no weapon at all, will prevail because God promised me they would not.

"No weapon that is formed against thee shall prosper; and every tongue that shall rise against thee in judgment thou shalt condemn. This is the heritage of the servants of the Lord, and their righteousness is of me, saith the Lord."

---Isaiah 54:17 (KJV)

I whispered "No weapon. No weapon." I noticed Donna staring at me out of the corner of my eye, but she knew what I was doing and just turned back to face the show.

For a few seconds, perhaps minutes, I was someplace else. I don't remember where, but I was gone. I rejoined reality as Judge Deborah Cantrell was briefing the jury on the counts.

"Harassment in the first degree," Judge Cantrell was instructing in an almost robotic formal tone.

"Means a pattern of intentional, substantial, and unreasonable intrusion in to the private life of a targeted person that serves no legitimate purpose and causes the person and would cause a reasonable person in his position to suffer mental or emotional distress. Harassment in the first degree may include, but is not limited to:

1. Following the targeted person as he moves from location to location.

2. Visual or physical contact that is initiated, maintained, or repeated after a person has been provided oral or written notice that the contact is unwanted or after the victim has filed an incident report with a law enforcement agency...."

I am not sure how long she went on for, but the words began to sound distant and muffed as if under water.

Then two officers walked him in. James looked calm; I might even say he looked confident, like he was certain that he would eventually just walk away from this.

In typical narcissistic form, I don't think he really believed that he would ever be made responsible for the things he did. He did not believe that he could ever be found guilty and be sent to prison for many years. This is the classic narcissist; living in an alternate state of reality.

The wolf, James' attorney, stood as James neared the desk with his hands cuffed behind his back, he paused and the big officer took his handcuffs off.

I don't know if it was deliberate that one of the officers to escort James happened to be a mountain of man, but he looked as though he could have snapped James in half.

James was six feet tall and a fit two-hundred pounds before he went to jail, but he looked like a child next to this police iron-man. The deputy reminded me of Lt. "Bubba" Skinner on the television series "In the Heat of the Night" with Carroll O'Connor. Not only was he tall, but his arms were easily the circumference of my waist.

Then I realized that in addition to Officer Bubba, what also made James look so small is that he *was* smaller. While the wrinkled, oversized brown suit that was an obvious *loaner* from the court or the jail, didn't help his feeble appearance, the fact was that he was just smaller.

He definitely had lost weight, a lot of it, and somehow, he shrank, or at least looked like he did. That six foot, two-hundred-pound frame looked every bit of five-nine or ten and maybe a hundred and fifty pounds.

As strong and confident as he was trying to look, and the *"I am a completely innocent man"* facade that he tried to project to the jury, may have worked on some people there, but I knew him. To me, he looked frail, timid, weak, and afraid, regardless of the mask he wore.

Following instructions from Judge Cantrell, the young female assistant prosecutor, who looked as if she just stepped out of law school, eager to try her first case, made the opening statement for the prosecution.

While I had my doubts, the rookie assistant proved to be every bit the skilled navigator of the courtroom. She was direct and methodically to the point and if she was nervous, then she would have made a great poker player, because I'm sure no one could tell.

Backing up the rookie and leading the team, was a seasoned veteran prosecutor from the Special Victims Unit.

On the other side, the defense attorney appeared poorly organized and talked entirely too long. I think he lost most of the jurors after just five minutes of his babbling.

The prosecuting team would present ten witnesses; several of whom were deputies who had arrested James at one time or another. A few were forensic analysts who scanned through over 10,000 incriminating pictures, google searches, and my personal information and documents that were found stored on James' computer and digital devices.

Finally, there was a direct eyewitness who saw James pushing the footlocker containing all of his firearms and weapons through the marsh and wooded area.

The prosecution strategically planned for Officer Jane and I to be the last two witnesses with me taking the stand last, just before the defense took over.

Of course, Jane and I were the heart and soul of the case. Jane described over a hundred instances of alarming evidence in excruciating detail and left jurors disturbed and the defense nervous.

While the defense team and James tried not to appear worried, I don't think I had as much luck as I sat quietly waiting for the State's attorney to call my name to take the stand.

I thought that I would be so scared and shaky on my way to the stand that my feet would sound like a drum roll on the cold tiled floor. However, once she called my name, a wave of overwhelming calm confidence swept over me. I knew the angels were by my side.

After the junior prosecutor presented the so-greeting cards James sent to me, which I identified and verified, she asked me to describe one of the nights that James had followed me, stalked me, in the literal definition of crime.

I would like to say that I gave a masterful performance, but it was nothing of the kind. As the truth came from my mouth and the thoughts of the account began to stream forth, the emotions poured out and so did the tears. While I wanted the jury to understand how vulnerable and defenseless I was at that time, I did not plan to bare my soul to the point of turning myself inside out, fully exposing the sensitive nerve endings of all of my emotions.

I thought about all of the years I spent rehearsing for this very moment, practicing my stoic face, and cool and calm demeanor to show that I was not some half-witted basket case. I was an educated, respectable, well-balanced member of society with a credible story. I needed to be cool and measured to prove my case.

If I came across as an emotionally flippant woman who turned every molehill into a mountain and became hysterical for the slightest reason, then of course it would look like all James did was approach me and I lost my mind.

I had my head down, drying tears with some tissues and not facing the jury, which I knew was a mistake. But I just could not face them right then. I didn't want to know what they were thinking about my loss of emotional control. So, I hid my head and planned to stay in that ostrich position for the remainder of the questioning.

However, it was not to be, as that young whippersnapper of an assistant prosecutor asked me a question; in fact, it was *the* question. It was the main question that I believe swayed the jury to truly understand me and see the truth.

The attorney used the power of the *pause* as effectively the most celebrated trial lawyers in the world, and then she asked,

"Dr. Anderson, could you please tell us when the defendant, James Oden" She paused as she turned to point at James.

"When *he* would follow you, stalk you, can you explain how that made you feel?"

"Whoa!" I thought. How do I answer this without completely breaking down and losing it? A lump the size of an orange formed in my throat and a chill ran through me followed by a hot flow of anger, then fear, as I recalled the incidents.

I figured it would be best if I just put this in as few words as I could. I knew I wouldn't last much longer up there.

"Well I..." I began with my head down, then raised it and looked toward the jury. I made sure to make eye contact with as many of them as I could as I said "I felt like a hunted animal!"

Looks of disgust, anger, repulsion, and disgrace came from every member of the jury as they all, in near perfect unison, turned and looked at James.

The defense presented their case and it quickly came and went. I say this because frankly, some of it, I barley remember. It seemed insignificant, menial, and trivial.

The defense attorney tried to discredit me to no avail, as his fiery darts at me ricocheted off *the Shield of Faith* from every answer that I gave directly from the *Belt of Truth*.

The wolf tried to confuse the jury, as is the way of the enemy because he is the author of confusion. But it would not be, as the *Sword of the Spirit* cut through the muck and mire of misunderstanding with both of its edges.

I remember that in the pre-trial, the wolf said that he had a rigorous, two-hour cross-examination of me planned, but if he did anything like that, it breezed by unnoticed.

Thursday, January 23, 2020, 8:30 A.M.
Trial Day 2

Satan Started Early

From the very moment I awoke, I knew it was going to be a very long day. Some of the little tiny things that happened, or should I say, went wrong, I won't even mention.

Everything and anything that the devil could mess with, he did so, in a morning of mishap after mishap, all appearing to be a swarm of random, unfortunate events. Yet, I knew better.

Before I allowed the frustration to wear my nerves to the bone, a powerful wave of victory washed over me. I knew that if the enemy was going to this much trouble to disrupt my morning in the hopes that I wouldn't show up for court, then the whole thing had to be on the right track.

If the devil thought that his man was going to get away with it and walk free, he would not have gone through the time and trouble of harassing me.

No, the devil was on the ropes and I smelled a conviction brewing like a pot of hot fresh coffee in the morning.

Like an hourglass, the line to enter the courthouse squeezed down to a crawl as nearly everyone went through the metal detector.

My youngest son, Anthony, and I were well behind most of the people we knew were also headed to Courtroom #3 on the second floor, while a few lawyers and officials zipped past around the side, not going through the metal detectors.

While most of them were ahead of us in the line, the jurors, at least some of them I recognized, to my surprise, were in the same slow moving line that we were in.

Anthony did a terrific job keeping my mind occupied with small talk about the future so I wouldn't lose it, as we both knew that it was very possible that the verdict would come today.

"No..." Anthony was saying. "I say you need to give it at least five years, mom. Five years, would be my call."

That was in response to my talking about selling my house a few years after all of this was over and traveling for a while. Anthony had a concern about me traveling alone so soon and suggested that I wait at least five years.

Bless his heart; but I thought that was ridiculously long. I didn't want to tell him that I had been thinking about going on a long trip within the next month.

"We'll talk about it later." We both agreed as I emptied my pockets and put everything including my handbag in the little blue bin.

Things finally came to order about 9:00 am and everyone took their proper places. Judge Cantrell sat quietly for a few seconds, glancing down at a small note in her hand every once in a while.

"It has come to my attention that the opinions of one of the jurors may have been compromised. " The judge said with a clear and scrutinizing look directly at me.

Anthony and I looked at each other in shock and then I turned towards Donna who also had a look on her face that also said, "What in the world does compromised mean?"

"Apparently," the judge continued. "One of the jurors overheard the victim and her male companion discussing the sentencing they believed appropriate for the defendant.

What!?   Bewilderment, clouded by anxiety mixed up in a ball of confusion is the only way to describe the moment as my mind raced about in all directions.

This is a mistrial. This is all the wolf needs, to have the case thrown out. He's going to go free. Just as those thoughts ran through my mind, I glanced toward James and he was staring at me. I looked up at the judge to see if she noticed him looking at me; the judge had ordered him not to turn around and look at anyone in the courtroom especially me!

The Judge never saw him and he just slowly turned back to face the front, but that wry, evil grin of his was still staring at me.

I turned toward Donna and she became my mother. Then the chopping of the helicopter grew louder "Vu-Vump-Vu-Vump!"

It must have been directly over the building. The police sirens joined in the chaos and flickering blue and orange lights danced in the forest.

A powerfully bright search light beamed down into the windows and lit up everything in the place like a frozen black and white photo.

My mom and sister started to go over to the windows, when I screamed "No!" Freezing them in their tracks.

"Get away for the windows! They could start shooting!"

The three of us cuddled on the floor in a corner when I heard my cell phone buzz. It was Investigator Jane Sloan.

"We lost…" I could barely hear her as she was trying to shout over the noise some of which was right where she was calling, she must have been in a police car.

"What?" I yelled back.

"We lost him in the woods!" She said frantically. "We don't know where he is. I'm coming to you and sending an office to your room! Take cover…hide until I…"

Click. The call disconnected.

Was that her, the phone or something else. My mom, sister and I just sat still, frozen.

Then there was loud thump on the door. Then another and another. The fourth time the door burst open to reveal James standing there with that big crossbow pointed at us.

Before we could even think, he fired the bow launching the arrow at us. It seemed to be traveling across the hotel room in slow motion and I braced to die.

But then I noticed the arrow wasn't coming directly at me, it was slightly skewed to my left...towards my mother.

I turned to her and she looked at me in horror and called my name.

"Makayla! Makayla!"

An elbow nudged me in the shoulder, then again a litter harder. "Makayla!" Then someone grabbed my shoulder and shook me as I turned and saw Donna on the courtroom bench beside me, staring at me with a look of concern.

"Makayla!" she yelled in a whisper. "Are you alight?"

"Ah...yes." I said as I came back to the present time. "I'm fine."

"Gosh," Donna said not quite convinced of my mental state. "Where were you just then? You certainly weren't here."

"Uh...I was at the hotel, before. With my mom and..." My court advocate was walking toward us. "Never mind." I said.

As she leaned over to me, I started to explain that the conversation with my son in the hallway had nothing to do with sentencing or even with James at all.

She nodded her head and told me to just be quiet and to not worry about it and she walked back to the front.

"Don't worry about it?" I thought. Is she nuts? I can't let this go. The devil was on his game and he was proving to be effective. Then the Holy Spirit injected Chronicles 20:17 into my mind.

"You will not have to fight this battle. Take up you positions;
stand firm and see the deliverance the Lord will give you,
Judah and Jerusalem. Do not be afraid; do not be discouraged.
Go out to face them tomorrow, and the
Lord will be with you."
---Chronicles 20:17 (NIV)

Yes. That's right, I thought. I don't have to fight this. I don't have to worry about this. No sooner than my renewed faith took root, Judge Cantrell asked the attorneys for both sides if they thought that the juror could continue as a juror with an unbiased opinion regardless of what she had overheard heard.

The assistant prosecutor immediately stood up and said yes, the prosecution had no problems with that juror continuing on the case.

The defense attorney slowly stood and I tried not to see him as the wolf he was. My son put his arm around me and Donna tightly grasped my hand.

To my shock and delight, he also agreed. The defense team had no issues with the juror.

"My God!" I thought. My God. Only He could have squashed that attempt to derail everything. All the wolf had to say was no and that would have been the end. That's it. Just a plain and simple no.

The judge told the bailiff to escort the jury into the courtroom and I praised God.

The Prosecution Rests

By 10:00 the prosecuting team prepared to play our last piece of evidence. It was a video of James under interrogation shortly after one of his multiple arrests.

During the pre-trial, the defense fought viciously to prevent allowing this video to be entered as evidence. They claimed that by doing so it would reveal discussions of past offenses committed by James and would therefore prejudice the jury to the crime he was now accused.

The prosecution said that the video was crucial in showing James' state of mind just after the assault, and that there was nothing in the video about previous crimes or arrests for harassment, assault, or stalking.

The young sharpshooting prosecutor Jessica was on her game, and the judge said she would allow the video to be played, as long as there was nothing about previous offenses.

The video was surreal. It was like watching a child adamantly denying that he ate any of the chocolate cake, and feeling proud of the fact that he is fooling his parents. All the while, the kid has chocolate smeared all over his face, shirt, and hands.

The faces of the jurors showed feelings of pity, sadness, and anger rolled up in one as James Oden made up story after story. I think what really got to them, was how he would change personalities in the middle of a sentence.

One minute he had me on a pedestal, musing about how much he loved me, and I supposedly loved him. He would explain how he felt afraid for me and only wanted to protect me.

Then a blink of an eye later, his eyes would flair up in a crazed looking haze, and an evil darkness would cover him, and he'd tell the detectives that I was the wicked witch of Biloxi in the flesh.

It was sad. It was insane.

I don't remember exactly what point the interrogator in the video was making, but he mentioned that James was out of jail on bond, and that did it.

Judge Cantrell immediately stopped the tape, admonished the prosecutors as if they were ten-year olds for allowing prejudicial information and ordered the bailiff to remove the jury from the courtroom.

Oh my God, I thought. Here we go again. The defense has yet another opportunity to motion for a mistrial.

I don't know exactly where I was, in my mind that is, during that hour or so that the judge and both legal teams argued the case for a mistrial. But I was not scared. I did not have another flash back and I did not pass out.

I just sat patiently and waited. I was tired. I was so tired; tired of that courtroom, tied of calling the police, tired of watching him get locked up, tired of praying. I was tired of everything. All of these years, I just wanted it all to be over.

They came to an agreement. The judge would not call a mistrial and the trial would continue; however, she declared the video inadmissible and it would be struck from the trial and the records as evidence.

When the jury was back in their seats, the Judge instructed them for a good twenty minutes about forgetting what they saw, and that they were not to consider anything in the video in making their decision on a verdict.

I thanked God and quietly asked that He forgive my brief lapse of faith.

The assistant prosecutor stood and declared "The prosecution rests."

The judge glanced at the defense attorneys.

"The defense rests, Your Honor." The wolf grudgingly said. The words caused him obvious pain to say.

"This court in in recess for lunch." Judge Cantrell said. "We will resume at 2:00 pm." The magistrate instructed and she stood and softly banged the gavel.

Closing Arguments

Everyone was back in their seats by exactly 2:00 as the legal teams prepared to present their closing arguments. I already had the feeling of being in a live television courtroom drama like the old Perry Mason, but I had no idea just how much more dramatic it would get.

Assistant Prosecutor Jessica got the ball rolling. She, along with three helpers who I figured were law interns, but in this context were more like stage-hands, set up the props for the prosecution.

The helpers at Jessica's theatrical direction strategically set up every single piece of physical evidence they had, as well as delivery systems to introduce even more powerful means of proving the case, all in preparation for the show. And what a show it was.

The prosecutor had a flip chart on her left, a laptop connected to a video projector to her right, and a huge white projection screen that covered the entire wall directly facing the jury.

Jessica's closing statement went on for over two hours as she meticulously detailed nearly every moment of the entire ordeal, starting from when James and I met.

She painfully dragged the jury through James' psychopathic behavior step by excruciating step, and brought them along as James crossed four state lines to set up a bizarre shrine to his victim, which the big screen eerily displayed in the slightly dimmed courtroom.

As the jury sat, disgusted by the image, with the click of Jessica's mouse, parts of my victim statement appeared on the screen beneath the shrine in big red letters.

"I am scared for my life"
"I planned my escape"
"I feel like a hunted animal"

The great Mark Twain once said

"The right word may be effective, but no word was ever as effective as a rightly timed pause."

Jessica must have known this as she once again, paused, and allowed the whole thing to sink in. The pause only lasted a few seconds I'm sure, but every second that ticked by, you could feel the weight of the insanity of James' thinking grow heavier.

Jessica latched on the last part of my statement on the screen and picked up a large, old grey bucket on one of the prop tables. She began slowly pacing in front of the jury carrying the bucket.

"Like an animal." Jessica said as though she were spitting the words out of her mouth.

"An animal. A hunted animal." She continued. "Do you know what that is like? Can you even imagine what it feels like to be hunted like an animal? Hunted by someone who is ready to use this..." and she violently shook the bucket.

The police confiscated the bucket from James' dive shop and apparently, James had filled it with dozens if not hundreds of large caliber bullets. The racket it made when she shook that bucket unnerved everybody in the court, but being just inches from the jury, some of them nearly jumped out of their skin.

"He hunted her like an animal," Jessica continued. "And why? After one of his arrests in 2018, he told us why. He proudly told the police why he felt he could do anything to her.

He said, "She is my wife. I don't know why she left me. I just love her."

A long powerful pause.

Jessica used the flip chart to remind the jurors that at the time of his arrest, James fled from the scene. He ran towards the power lines, swam across the marsh, and limped through the wooded area where he had hidden the crossbows, rifles, and guns. She used a pointer to trace every movement on the map.

Finally, she walked over to face the jury up close and said, "Now it is your job to find the defendant guilty of stalking." She sat down.

The only word I could think of was *masterful*.

The look on the faces of most of the jurors said how they felt about the defense's closing arguments as he began.

There wasn't a single character witness who could say one positive thing about the defendant. Not a single expert witness, which I was expecting to hear. But then again, the state has the burden of proof and must clearly show the facts. The only thing the defense has to plant is doubt.

The defense's closing argument looked disorganized and unplanned. He often repeated himself and would stare at his notes for extended periods of time, and then would ramble on seemingly aimlessly, but somehow he managed to go on for two hours as well.

The Verdict

Judge Deborah Cantrell once again, explained to the jury the precise legal definitions of the words, "harassment" and "stalking"; the crimes for which James stood accused.

She further explained that harassment carries a prison term of one to five years and stalking was punishable by one to up to fifteen years in prison. The judge very carefully and methodically continued to give the jury their detailed instructions and then dismissed them to deliberate. It was 6:30 pm.

The jury went to a room to deliberate, the Judge moved to her chambers and Donna, her husband, my son, and I, like so many others in the courtroom, stepped out into the hallway and found wooden benches. Our choices where to stay in the courtroom and wait for a verdict that would hopefully come that night, or to sit in the hallway. To take a quick break and find restrooms, we took to the hallway first.

James Oden went back to his five by ten foot cell and the courthouse went on complete lockdown; no one could enter or leave the building.

After a little while, Donna and I went back into the courtroom, and I began to prepare, or rather finish my victim statement.

By 8:30 pm I began to wonder what would happen if the jury did not come to a verdict that night. Would we stay here all night? The judge never actually mentioned the word *sequestered*.

We were all back in our seats in the courtroom, when I stepped out to get a sip of the horribly tasting, yet pleasingly cold water, from the water fountain in the hallway.

I sat down on the bench near the fountain and again began to think about life if James was not convicted.

At 8:45, I thought I heard a shout in the courtroom and started to walk toward the double-doors when the doors burst open and the bailiff stuck his head out.

"The jury has reached a verdict!" he announced to everyone in the area. "The jury has reached a verdict and court will resume momentarily."

If I had big knife, I believe I could have literally cut a slice of the air, as the tension and the mood, were thick and heavy.

The jury began to enter and take their seats and I watched them. I desperately tried to remember what one of those TV-courtroom shows said about what it meant when the jurors looked at you and when they did not.

Did it mean that they voted in your favor when they looked at you when they came back from deliberating? Or was it the other way around?

"Has the jury reached a verdict?" Judge Cantrell asked.

A short, petite Hispanic woman, the spokesperson for the jury, seated at the front and nearest the judge, stood.

"We have your honor."

The judge nodded to the bailiff who accepted a folded piece of paper from the spokeswoman and handed it to the judge. The judge unfolded the paper and took a quick glance at it and refolded it and said

"What say you?"

"We the jurors..." the Hispanic woman began. She stared straight at the judge and did not move her head in any other direction. So much for TV, I thought.

"...find the defendant, James Oden..." I don't think she actually paused here, but it seemed like it took forever for those next words to fall from her mouth.

"...Guilty of harassment in the first degree."

A grey emotional cloud surrounded me has I was happy, I knew I was elated, but I don't know, I felt some tinge of disappointment as well.

As Donna and my son or both were shaking me and patting me on my back and shoulders, and saying something to me, I wondered about the stalking. Why not guilty of the stalking? I later found out that for a guilty verdict on the stalking meant that he would have had to assault me, or kidnap me, or rape me, or something. That didn't make any sense to me.

As the judge was thanking the jury, Donna had grabbed my hand again, and squeezing it, drew my eyes to hers. One look at the smile, the relief on her face brought me back to the reality of the moment.

That reality was that any guilty verdict meant that James Oden would be spending several years in prison.

Before excusing the jury, the judge welcomed them to stay for the sentencing if they wished and nine of the twelve did.

After statements and recommendations from both the prosecution and the defense, it was my turn. I was able to read my victims statement.

I walked up to the front of the courtroom and took the podium in front of the judge and between the two legal teams. I looked over at those who had remained from the jury and then back at the judge.

I had rehearsed this moment in my mind so many times. So many times, I had thought of this very minute and thought of the day James would be found guilty of his crimes against me, and I was certain that, when the moment finally came, I would be a nervous wreck.

To my surprise, I was as calm as ever. I was so calm and relaxed that I wondered if it was really me. I think that was because I had also practiced trying not to sound wild and too emotional. I didn't want to come off sounding unbalanced. Then I realized, it's over. That maniac is already convicted. I'm just going to share the truth. That is exactly what I did.

Honorable Judge,

Thank you for allowing me to read my victim statement.

I regret ever meeting and bringing James Oden into my life, my home and my precious families' lives.

The actions of James Oden have completely impacted and changed my life. In these last 2-3 days, the court has heard about some the "bad acts". I would rather call them "monstrous acts".

He invaded every aspect of my life. He hacked my social media, utility account, and even my online banking account. He repeatedly hacked my emails and even learned about a cruise trip to the Caribbean. He purchased the same cruise trip!

I thank God every day, that I spotted him at the Miami, FL cruise terminal. Fortunately, the captain of the ship made the right call and had James Oden escorted off the terminal. Whatever plot he had planned did not succeed. He returned from his trip and targets my frail mother and sister. On her way to church, my sister was unable to properly brake her car.

Among other monstrous acts, he threw carpenter nails in my mother's driveway. He slashed my friend's tires.

Your honor, the actions of James Oden have left me in a catatonic state. I will always share my nightmare with others, but more importantly, that I am here today because of God's beautiful grace.

I have been a victim for 6 years, but tonight at 9pm, I am a survivor!

Silence.

I was so cool and calm; I half expected a small applause. Instead, I got silence and melancholy faces. It was then I realized that I had been selfish in my thinking.

My story was not just *my* story. My victim statement was not just for me. Yes, the details were about me, but the whole story, the entire six-year long ordeal was about a lot more than just me.

The story was about the tribulation of thousands of women and men who would come after me. The statement was about several people in the courtroom who remained silent, while they cried internally for themselves, or a loved one who they knew was going through the nightmare, someone who was living the torment at that very moment.

The victim statement was for those innocent victims who would wear a wide-eyed, bushy-tailed, unsuspecting vail of naivety, all the way to the slaughter.

The statement was for you. The story was for you reading this book right now and saying to yourself

"No, my man is not like that. What happened the other night will never happen again."

As I took my seat, Judge Cantrell spoke and said something I will never forget.

She said, "Mr. Oden needs to be removed from society and Ms. Anderson. He is a danger and I strongly recommend that he seek mental assistance in our correctional facility."

Just then, the weight that I had not realized had been on my shoulders for years, lifted, and I stood taller in my seat. I felt the power. All of my power had come back, full circle.

"Mr. James Oden" the judge said as she brandished the gavel in her right hand.

"I hereby sentence you are to serve five consecutive years in the South Carolina Correctional Department. Good luck to you."

Epilogue

This story, as painful as it has been at times, was never really about James. The testimony was not even about me, nor was it all about informing you about the horrors and realties of stalking.

This story was really about what God has done for my family and me. God has protected us and was with me through this very dark moment in my life. Like I said, when your life is in a mess, make the mess your message!

God bless you!

STALKING VICTIM RESOURCES

Are you or have you been harassed by a stalker? Are you experiencing domestic or intimate partner abuse? Below are several resources and ideas that may help. Remember, your P.O.W.E.R.; at some point, you must Open up and reach out and to someone. Do it now.

The Federal Bureau of Investigation - Internet Crime Complaint Center

Also known as the IC3 (complaints can be criminal or civil). Victims can file a complaint on this website here **IC3** (https://www.ic3.gov)

I had to fill out five reports, but they finally assigned my case to a local investigator.

Public, Police & Public Sector ("P3")

On a local level, most counties have an online tip form. A victim can submit their complaints online using an app called "P3 Tips." It's the public, police, and public sector working together to solve and prevent crimes.

Your Local Police Department or Magistrate

Filing suspicious activities (unknown phone calls, email hacking, being followed, etc.) you must report! This is vital! It is tiresome sometimes, but you have to build your case.

Document Everything

Write everything down and take lots of pictures. Learn to screen shot pictures on your cell phone. This is how I collected all of my evidence. Learn to keep it in chronological order.

Restraining Orders

A Restraining Order or Order of Protection are a great way to document what is happening and give you a little protection. There are a few different types and provisions of restraining orders. You can file these yourself or see an attorney.

1. **No Trespassing Order:** Prohibits the criminal from entering or coming within certain radius of your property.
2. **Emergency Order of Protection:** When the threat is imminent and serious, most states will issue one of these almost immediately.

3. **No Contact Provision**: Prohibits the abuser from calling, texting, emailing, stalking, attacking, hitting, or disturbing you.

4. **Peaceful Contact Provision**: Permits the abuser to peacefully communicate with you for limited reasons, including care and transfer for visitation of their child.

5. **Stay Away Provision**: Orders the abuser to stay at least a certain number of yards or feet away from you or your home, job, school, and car. The stay-away distance can vary by state, judge, or the lethality of the situation, but is often at least 100 yards or 300 feet. Unlike the no trespassing order prohibiting the abuser from your property, this provision can apply to almost anywhere

6. **Move-Out Provision**: Requires the stalker to move out of a residence that you share.

7. **Firearms Provision**: Requires the abuser to surrender any guns he or she possesses or bars the abuser from purchasing a firearm.

8. **Counseling Provision**: Orders the abuser to attend counseling, such as batterer's intervention or anger management.

Most of these protection orders are temporary, lasting six months to a year. However, you can apply for a permanent order when there are several stalking, harassment, or abuse charges. I got a permanent order of protection.

9. **Stalking Resource Centers:** There are a ton of resources centers around the country. While they differ in their overall mission or focus, each can be very helpful. Check them out and see what best fits your case and circumstances. You can just Google "stalking resource centers," or "domestic violence protection," or something of the sort. In the meantime, here are a few to get your started:

   a. <u>Stalking Resource Center, National Center for Victims of Crime</u> (https://www.legalmomentum.org)

   b. <u>National Center for Victims of Crime</u> (https://victimsofcrime.org)

   c. <u>Safe Horizon</u> (https://www.safehorizon.org)

   d. <u>SPARC (Stalking Prevention. Awareness and Resources Center)</u> (https://www.stalkingawareness.org)

    e. <u>**NSVRC (National Sexual Violence Resource Center)**</u> (https://www.nsvrc.org)

    f. <u>**Stalking Resource Center**</u> **(https://www.facebook.com/StalkingResourceCenter)**

Contact Me

I thank you for reading my book and pray that something that you read, or discovered, something in it that will help you get through it, and of course, will help you get your power back.

Please feel free to contact me personally for comments or questions, or just to have a shoulder to lean on of someone who knows what you are going through.

DrMakaylaAnderson@yahoo.com

Thank you and God bless you!

Dr. Makayla Anderson

Dr. Makayla Anderson